Successful
Team Building
Through TA

Successful Team Building Through TA

Dudley Bennett

amacom *A DIVISION OF*
AMERICAN MANAGEMENT ASSOCIATIONS

HD
58.7
.B46

Library of Congress Cataloging in Publication Data

Bennett, Dudley.
   Successful team building through TA.

   Includes index.
   1. Organizational behavior. 2. Transactional
analysis. 3. Organizational change. I. Title.
HD58.7.B46   658.4'036   80-65869
ISBN 0-8144-5607-3

First Printing

Preface

The yellow pads I write on are often spotted with and smell of machine oil and lignin. The insights of this book were developed in discussions that took place in board rooms, training centers, tool cribs, dust-free rooms, and on shop floors. Computer manufacturing, banking, papermaking, international air travel, heavy manufacturing, and marketing were the environments for our learnings. The clients to whom I owe so much cannot be mentioned by name; their openness and shared confidences made the entire effort possible.

This book is a contribution to the literature on Transactional Analysis and organizational development. It is about business and industrial organizations and reports my efforts of the last ten years assisting workers at all levels to see themselves, others, and the company in a new way. Of the more than 50 companies I worked with, approximately one-third were organized and involved in collective bargaining. Using new-style assumptions and strategies, we found forces present in both labor and management moving them toward significantly higher levels of collaboration within the tension of the adversary relationship. In this period I also worked with two school systems. Although the educators reported satisfaction with the outcome, I was less pleased with the results. Educational systems present special problems today.

The basic conceptional apparatus of Transactional Analysis was developed by Eric Berne in the late 1950s and through the 1960s. The indebtedness of all of us to this great innovator is inestimable. Us lesser folk can see much farther standing on the shoulders of great men. I am also indebted to those who spent time with Berne and later made their own contributions to the TA thought system. Claude Steiner and Jacqui Schiff, whom I know only through their writings, made timely contributions to my thinking as I struggled with a particularly resistant organizational impasse. I have tried in every case to report my indebtedness to those on whose shoulders I stand. When ideas are shared in professional group discussions over many years, their origin is sometimes lost. Should someone see an idea here he or she believes was first his or hers, I cheerfully apologize in advance.

I wish to report the good contribution of my colleague Karen Davis. In our work together we have spent many hours planning, executing, and evaluating interventions into a variety of business organizations. Her unfailing good cheer, ease with life, willingness to take risks, and fine education have made an important contribution to my work and thinking. Karen made a number of useful additions to the "Self-Scoring Profiles of Organizational Characteristics," found in Chapter 3. It is one of the diagnostic instruments we use.

I am pleased to record the names of friends who have been open with themselves and willing to share their knowledge: Denny Thomas, Roger Armstrong, Dave Thomas, Mike Griffith, Jonas Aarons, Noel Frizel, Paul Pieschel, Connie Firm, Linda Wise, and Charles Whigham. I am proud to have such friends. Werner Erhard has made a recognizable contribution to my life and work. The est training program clarified and gave an emotional lift to some ideas I had been struggling with. Graduates will recognize some statements of social ideas that came out of the training. I was charmed by them.

To my wife and co-worker, Margaret Ann, belongs credit for

the production aspect of the book. Her unflagging patience in retyping, checking references, and consulting the dictionary have benefited every page. Our children, Paul, Martha, and Sarah, remain one of our chief joys.

In the course of my work, there were things I wanted managers and workers to know that I found I could not tell them. Often, there just wasn't time or the situation was inappropriate. I wanted to give them the whole picture, to set down in one place the many ideas we bring to any development effort. That is one of the reasons I was impelled to write this book. Many people found *TA and the Manager* helpful and got in touch with me on the basis of what they found there. This book complements the earlier one. Each contains some material not found in the other. Hopefully, they will be side by side on your reference shelf.

Teams, work groups, divisions, and companies invite me into their life on the expectation I will be helpful to them. I seek to be responsible to them by thinking accurately, working carefully, modeling support behavior and openness, and faithfully recording learnings. Social change can become very complex—and nothing less, in my view, will do. Our learnings are based on our failures as well as successes. Our failures, which we have considered in detail, are not so recorded here. They would feed unproductive assumptions, confirm cynicism, and possibly dissuade some from the effort. Repetition is a sound learning tool. I have used it freely where I judge understanding a concept to be necessary to the entire development process.

The growing dysfunction of American social institutions must be obvious to even the most casual viewer. While I suspect the changes are not all bad, I cannot help being saddened by the growing failures of family, education, and politics. For hundreds of years we have known how to teach children to read, yet we "graduate" students after 12 years of schooling who can't read. Not everything about the past was better, and we are not without hope for the future. We have much work to do on improving social life.

During the recent gas "crisis" editorial writers wrung their hands over the country's ominous future because of the failures of Washington. If only we had a more effective President, they argued, the crisis would be solved. Such a position is gamey ("If It Weren't for Them") and wrongheaded. The people, not the politicians, are the hope for the future. True, the executive officer can make things much better or much worse, but whether we undertake a program of development in a country or in a company, we end up by empowering the workers. That workers have no expectation of this is only part of the problem. We can begin in no better way than by helping them understand their own elegance and the integrity of social life.

I wish this book to contribute to a most critical discussion today: What does it take to make our social systems run better? I believe in the free-market philosophy. It seems to me the best way to maximize both individual and group potential. I wish to support those who understand human life as social. I stand beside all those who work together to better social institutions.

DUDLEY BENNETT

Contents

Successful Team Building Through TA

1
Old Style–New Style

I first heard the old style–new style paradigm in 1965.* Many managers have found it helpful in understanding why organizations that were effective in the industrial age function less well in the technological era. Old style is the authority-obedient, power-on, top-down management system, which is usually visualized as a pyramid. Power was seen to be on top and filtered down through the ranks. Power was the mode of operation, fear the control, and being separated the ultimate punishment. The models were the church and the army, whose origins belong to the dim mists of the past. Anything that survived so long and was so consequential had argued its own validity. Resistance to change from old-style managers is usually framed in these terms: "We've always done it this way," and "Always stick with the tried and true."

OLD-STYLE SKILLS

What skills made it possible for old-style systems to operate? A skill is something that can be learned. Leadership was the first skill. This is the ability to decide, delegate, control, and evaluate those who report to you. Leaders, it was understood,

* It was used by Herb Shepard at the NTL Program for Specialists in Organizational Development at Bethel, Maine.

were good, clean, kind, brave, and true. You deserved to be a leader because you were the best. Rank and competence were thought to be directly related. "Go it alone," "Survive," "Separate the men from the boys," and "If you can't stand the heat, stay out of the kitchen" were admonitions used in a variety of ways to encourage continuance on the lonely path.

The question was seriously discussed: Are leaders made or born? The assumption was that if the leader was good, the system was benevolent. Workers could then commit themselves to supporting it, hoping they might one day be called to higher responsibility. Stress was placed on education as a way of proving oneself deserving of greater responsibility, with the payoff of greater status among one's peers and friends. The payoff was symbolized by improved working conditions. The size of the office, its location and window dimensions, and the relative distance between the rug and the wall became issues of great importance. Seeing this, one wag commented: "The only difference between men and boys is the price of the toys they play with."

Along with leadership came the skill of followership. If workers hoped to be leaders, it was argued they first had to learn to be followers. Such policy was designed to ensure that things didn't change much. If a worker hoped to succeed, the necessary skill was acquiescence: "Stay in line," "Go along," and "Don't make waves." By assuming the culture and coloring of the organization, a worker could hope someday to achieve preeminence. It is not at all strange to hear someone referred to as a "real Ford sort of guy," or "simply not IBM." Anyone different, anyone who didn't go along or didn't seem to fit, was suspect.

The system worked well enough in a day when the external environment was stable. In those earlier days, an executive could spend a lifetime building a role relationship with the community. The local banker, for example, knew who he was and how to think about himself. Once he had acquired the basic skills of managing an investment portfolio, he had it made. Members of the community likewise knew what to expect from him and how to work with him. Today, with the increased rate of social change, these role relationships are strained. Where society was once constant and slow to change, it is now chaotic and ambiguous. Banking is in revolution. Bankers have constantly to shift their perspective, learn new technology, and be ready to abandon anything that is not cost-effective. In short, they need new behavioral skills. The shift is from "soldiering" to problem solving, from rigidity to flexibility, from the medium to the message. In terms of organizational dynamics, it is from bureaucratic to familial.

The influence of soldiering on the boss is noteworthy. Subordinates sought to please him, to see his ideas with special clarity, to shield him from bad news, to anticipate his needs, to support the notion that he made more sense than the average person. His anger was more just, his success/failure ratio better than anyone else's, his jokes funnier, and his questions more penetrating. Under such treatment the quality of decision making is degraded. I have seen such servility create an aura of unreality in the executive suite. Sometimes, despite their protestations, I was convinced subordinates' motivations were malign.

In the old-style organization, few are shepherds, many are sheep. Few are officers, many are privates. Few are teachers, many are students. Few are managers, many are workers. All of these are relationships in which a small number hold the resource that is granted to a few upon payment of a certain obedience. Under the old style, nonconformity was seen as uncivil, unsocial, and rebellious. The response to it was repression. A supervisor said to me recently: "If we can't control workers with money or the fear of the loss of it, and we can't hit them with a stick, how are we going to keep this plant running?"

Workers are rebelling today against a diminished humanity

associated with old-style going along. "I am tired of the dog-and-pony show," they say. "I am a person; I have a contribution to make and feelings to share. My vision of a humane and just society is more important than your need for control."

Competitiveness was another old-style skill. The assumption was that since people were essentially flawed, they could not be trusted. If you left them alone, they would wander off, go fishing, become ineffectual, or worse. So it was deemed necessary to pit people against each other in the contest for rewards and status. Thus we were taught from a young age to take care of "old number one." Only the best rise to the top, we were enjoined. In school years ago, when I had trouble with an arithmetic problem, I couldn't lean over to the person next to me and say, "Help me solve this problem." That would be cheating. Instead of seeing my neighbor as a resource for problem solving, I was cautioned not to get too friendly. "It might cause problems." When competition reaches the point where it causes fear and distrust, communication and relationships begin to break down.

A friend of mine heads a lab of 20 scientists. He reports, "I've Ph.D.s in physics from the best schools in the country, including MIT, Cal Tech, and Chicago. Recent graduates 27 years old arrive at the lab as tired little old men who do not know how to think." This is another consequence of old-style thinking. As students, these scientists were put in a Skinner box where they were rewarded when they responded to the stimuli of the system. The process, of course, was arduous and complex. Sometimes equations covered the blackboard wall to wall, but the process remained simple stimulus and response. The outcome was thinking that was characteristically analytical and convergent.

Today we need leaders whose thinking is expansive and divergent. We need men and women who can dream dreams—and old-style schools turn out those who see life as linear. For want of dreams, the prophet warns, a people die. This narrow-

ing of perspective, this inability to think in larger terms, is
what threatens many social systems.

Another old-style skill was impersonality. Feelings were
something that got in the way of business. They were discom-
fiting, difficult, frightening, a hindrance to order. Impersonality was seen as essential. But when we deny, distort, and repress feelings, we destroy that which is human. Without feelings available to us, we tolerate anything. There is no atrocity
we cannot be comfortable with. The dysfunction for social systems becomes clear.

In the new age, on the "eighth day" nothing but fully operative beings with feelings available will do. The single most
important factor in creating "can do" teams is shared member
trust. You know what trust is? It's a feeling. That for which
there was no room in old-style systems is that upon which
hinge the possibilities of the future—the ability to trust, be
creative and open, and team with others.

An old-style manager's assumptions about workers on the
whole was negative. In a system based on control through fear,
it fit handily to have a diminished view of workers. Those to be
controlled were viewed as indifferent to their own mental and
emotional health. The impossibility of starting with the assumption that "people are no damned good" and then attempting to create a powerful business system escaped old-stylers.
The struggle to create a rational system out of presumed irrational individuals produces many of the strange kinds of organizational behavior with which we are so familiar.

Out of the old style there comes a drumbeat of inquiries from
hapless managers about communication, productivity, motivation. The second-most-reproduced article ever from the *Har-
vard Business Review* is Fred Herzberg's "One More Time: How
Do You Motivate Employees?" Questions formulated on old-
style assumptions foreordain managers to games and politics.
The standard definition of management is "getting work done
through others." It seems to make so much sense.

In an old-style setting it becomes more of the traditional "doing people something." Many managers have not yet seen the trap they create for themselves by cynicism. New-style assumptions about people begin to unpack all that was distasteful and counterproductive. The truth is people are all right the way they are. The task is not to change them. People have all the resources they need to solve the problems social life presents to them. They are not somehow so flawed that they can't resolve the problems they create for themselves. Whatever they have the ability to create they have the competence to resolve. Their problem-creating capacity is not somehow dangerously greater than their problem-solving ability, so that they are a fatal threat to themselves.

Are there not people who are a threat to themselves and others? To be sure. For a complex set of personal and social reasons some take to themselves destructive scripts. Both the roots and expression of pathological behavior are remediable with the application of special techniques in which TA in the hands of therapists has been spectacularly successful. Behavior distributes in the familiar bell curve. We are concerned here with that 85 percent of behavior that is characteristic of the vast majority of people, behavior that is described as normal.

My experience convinces me people have more than enough resources to do what has to be done to meet their life challenges. Human beings are, I believe, the highest form of natural life. The reports from the astro and particle physicists are astonishing. They describe a world of haunting beauty, of meaningful structure and power. It can only be described as elegant. There is no reason to believe we do not participate in this bounty. Scientists now say we use only a minuscule percentage of our intelligence. We have awesome potential, but we are only beginning to get in touch with it. The first step is to see that's so.

For too long we have been taught by our leaders to derogate

ourselves, to view ourselves as violent, lazy, selfish, and other bad things. Our leaders would wring their hands and lament the sad state of human affairs. We overlooked the fact that they benefited by the shared distress they perceived. Those who manned the levers of power of old-style organizations had an investment in our self-abnegation. They believed their cynicism, to be sure. Our natural unruliness, they surmised, could get out of hand and industrial society wouldn't work. So they kept alive the idea that deep down people were really sinners. "Total depravity" was the name of the doctrine.

Wasn't it difficult to maintain such a negative view of human nature as we entered the technological age? To be sure. Walking on the moon was but one of a myriad dazzling accomplishments that would have astonished Croesus not so many centuries ago. These accomplishments portend great hope, excitement, and dignity for mankind. Old-style leaders have long reminded us of our bloody history and the great distance between our prayers, our pretensions, and our actual history. What they didn't see was their own involvement in it. They enhanced their position by fostering our dependency. It was our leaders who too readily saw the necessity of fighting wars. Often, but not always, it was their wars we fought. We who had so little to recommend us.

Do managers still have so little hope for workers? Yes. Some do. This is doubly sad because divided, all are open to exploitation by those on the lunatic fringes, both left and right. Revolutionaries, observing us, create the myth that there is an irreconcilable gulf between managers and laborers. Our interests, they say, are inimical. "Managers treat workers like dogs—you can read it in the newspapers every week," they contend. And workers hold off management's depredations only with the support of unions and friendly politicians.

The supposed natural antipathy between management and labor is a myth. Those who push it are using the "big lie" tactic. If your lie is bold enough and told with conviction, people will believe it. After all, nobody could lie about something so important. Old-style managers mindlessly support revolutionary demagoguery in the way they treat each other and workers. We give support for others' bad ideas about us. Since nobody gains from the false war between management and labor, you'd think we would wise up. Many have, and that's what this book is about: those who have discovered that labor and management have many mutual interests. Nothing else makes sense. Nothing else works.

Is there more? Yes. Terrorism is rising. Advanced societies are vulnerable because of their complexity and interdependence. Senior managers more and more have to make contingency plans for improbabilities like "kneecapping," bombing, kidnapping, and political murder. Those against us have carried the idea of "total depravity" to its furthest limit. They no longer value individual life. Whatever they claim their motivations to be, absurdity is piled on absurdity when they wantonly waste life. Denying the value of the individual, they "think nothing of slaughtering individuals by the tens and hundreds when they are out of power, and by the millions when they control the state." *

Nothing in life means nothing. Whatever happens we create. Terrorism is created by postindustrial society. The sense of rootlessness, meaninglessness, and anomie that is so much a part of our society creates a deep despair that issues in lawlessness and self-destruction. Such behavior has been characteristic of periods of transition. And we are in such a period, going from the industrial to the technological age. The task of management is to move companies from the old style, which was suitable for the great industrial period, to a new style congruent with a period in which there is an explosion of knowledge.

Many managers see this and have begun training and de-

---

* Northrup Buechner, letter to *The New York Times,* May 21, 1978.

velopment activities to bring the transition about. Others, too far gone looking the other way, hope to avoid change and maintain the status quo until retirement. Some managers see that new challenges call for new strategies but wait for the opportune time. Others, indifferent to themselves, others, and society, seem bent on riding their organizations into the ground like a streamlined brick. This is far too frequent. Warren Bennis withdrew a couple of years ago as president of the University of Cincinnati and in a public address made a statement that at first seemed only hyperbole. "Mankind," he said, "faces three scourges which threaten all life: famine, nuclear holocaust, and the failure of management." The more I think about it, the more true it seems.

OLD-STYLE ASSUMPTIONS

What does the old-style manager hold to be true about workers? Observation and reflection over the years have produced a horrifying list. Given what most people assume about themselves, others, and social life, it's not surprising that companies have trouble functioning. Douglas McGregor covered the same ground years ago.*

The list shows us what we have to do. We have our work cut out for us. Table 1 compares old-style assumptions about workers with their new-style counterparts.

If people are treated in the old-style way as lazy, dependent, and irresponsible, they tend to become so. Unfortunately, workers too easily accept old-style derogations about themselves. When told they are inferior and without worth, they tend to accept it as an objective fact. It is an early goal of a new-style development program to get workers to reevaluate their as-

* Douglas McGregor, *The Human Side of Enterprise* (New York: McGraw-Hill, 1961).

Table 1. Assumptions about workers.

Old-Style Assumptions	New-Style Assumptions
1. By nature workers prefer to do nothing. Work is bad and to be avoided as much as possible. Really fortunate people never have to work. The best thing about work is that it makes doing nothing possible.	1. People want to be active and work, especially when it means accomplishment, contribution to others, responsibility, recognition, and advancement. The task is not to motivate people to work but to remove those things in the structure of work that demotivate them. Work itself motivates. Not to work is debilitating. Leisure is preferable to work only when leisure provides an opportunity to do better work.
2. People want to be left alone and prefer not to relate to others. Models for them are the wealthy who can do what they want when they want to.	2. People's highest achievements are always the consequence of social action (teamwork). Not to be related to others is a source of pain and sickness.
3. Workers return to work mostly because they need money and seek to gain status with friends. Their motives are negative.	3. People welcome work because of the many satisfactions it makes available to them: pleasure in being with friends; challenge of new problems; pride in success; enjoyment of learning; bonding that comes from joint effort; stimulation of the new.
4. Fear is the mode of social control and the force that increases productivity: fear of being passed over, ridiculed, or even fired. Successful managers skillfully prey on these fears to get their jobs done.	4. Workers are motivated by pride, the desire to achieve, and the need to belong and to grow personally and professionally. This is what keeps workers productive. The skillful manager enables workers to meet their personal goals while achieving the company mission.
5. Workers remain children all their lives, unconcerned about their mental and emotional growth. They are unable to think for themselves, take	5. People mature beyond childhood at different rates. They always desire greater self-control, self-respect, and self-fulfillment. Work is their primary

Table 1. (Continued)

Old-Style Assumptions	New-Style Assumptions
the long view, or be concerned with matters beyond their immediate self-interest.	source of mental, emotional, and spiritual development.
6. People are dependent on good leadership. Although they appreciate being treated with respect, sometimes the carrot must be replaced with the stick.	6. Workers are able to work independently to define and solve problems. They can devise new work methods and improve old ones. They crave authentic relationships with fellow workers.
7. Workers cannot think.	7. Given the opportunity to improve their intelligence, there is no limit to workers' mental development. Using sound tools and models, they can take charge of their own development and free themselves from the need for teachers.
8. Policy is not workers' business.	8. People naturally seek to give meaning to their lives and to widen their understanding. Their cognitive hunger is expressed in concern about issues of work, community, family, country, and church. They have a statement to make.
9. Workers need close supervision.	9. Every worker is a manager. It is the manager's task to give his or her job away by continually expanding the self-direction and self-control of subordinates. Problem solving always moves downward and outward.
10. Work must be broken down into the simplest units of time and motion.	10. Boredom is painful. Workers want to expand their capabilities and grasp the meaning of their part in the larger whole. They enjoy new experiences and respond positively to job enrichment.

Table 1. (Continued)

Old-Style Assumptions	New-Style Assumptions
11. Work comes first and only those individuals should be hired who can fit into the job.	11. Workers come first. Whenever possible, jobs are designed and fitted to people. Workers themselves are a constant resource for work enrichment activities.
12. You can't change people.	12. Workers want to grow. It is their primary source of joy. It is never too late to start anew. The only failure is the failure to learn.
13. People can't be trusted. Never turn your back on workers. They welcome any opportunity to rip you off.	13. Authentic, direct, game-free relationships generate trust, openness, and support behavior in people. People are eager to "team up" to accomplish tasks that have meaning for them. Workers show their health when they resist abuse.

Fred Herzberg et al., *The Motivation to Work* (New York: John Wiley & Sons, 1959), pp. 81ff.

sumptions about themselves and others and to help them adopt a more sanguine view.

The success of a change program will be limited if workers continue to believe they are incapable of change and improvement. If workers are treated as responsible, growth-oriented, independent, and goal-achieving, they tend to become so. This is the basis of all efforts to create a new culture where new-style behavior is first allowed, then encouraged, and finally rewarded. If the program begins with a defeatist attitude, there can be little hope for success. Those people who are responsible for training and development will have many occasions to remind themselves of their operative assumptions about people.

What can be done if people don't want to change? Nothing

directly. New-style programs seek to create the space that allows individuals to grow. Some workers will try small steps in new behavior and, if they are successful, attempt a few more. Others welcome the opportunity to get unstuck and immediately jump to a new plateau of success. A few seize the opportunity to drain all the program's resources and zip far ahead, looking for new insights and strengths.

Some managers, out of suspicion and cynicism, will resist. They will attempt to prove the program wrong and to have it removed. To neutralize their efforts, senior managers must be warned early that this will happen. If the resisters cling too tightly to their positions and are in important places, the program may have to be abandoned until the situation is more propitious. Often because the program has successes with many workers and achieves its business goals, even the doubting Thomases come along. Occasionally, some diehards find it easier to leave the company than to confront the new-style challenges of openness and candor.

OLD-STYLE CONSEQUENCES

What are some of the consequences of old-style management? What processes do we typically find in authority-obedient systems?

1. *Synergism is replaced by canceling out.* The natural forces in social life are paired in an agonist–antagonist relationship. The human body contains a multitude of examples. An extensor muscle when it contracts is automatically checked and controlled by the simultaneous expansion of the flexor muscles. This balance of action and reaction allows even, controlled, and powerful action. Without this careful balance, actions would be erratic and useless. With forces balanced, the total effect is greater than the sum of each force taken separately. When

people act in concert with one another, they enhance their effect. Two and two doesn't equal four but six, seven, or eight. Or else what is love all about? This is synergism.

When people are separated from each other and encapsulated in their own "acts," they tend to atrophy. They find it increasingly difficult to enter complex relationships that demand doing, thinking, and feeling. In old-style organizations, people tend to view each other competitively. Since rewards are considered scarce, others are seen as obstacles to one's own success. This "he's breathing the air I should be breathing" attitude obviates the possibility of collaboration.

Much of old-style management is really management by secrecy. If you don't know what I'm doing, you can't take credit for my work or, alternatively, help me fail. In such an environment, behavior tends to be reduced to games. A opens and B doubles. C advances and D counters. E acts and F reacts.

2. *Political behavior unrelated to organizational goals is highly visible.* This has two aspects. One is the great amount of energy spent in defensive behavior unrelated to company goals. When management by secrecy prevails, withholding behavior comes into prominence. The rules for destructive fighting are:

- Never state your own position clearly; only attack others' ideas.
- Always anticipate the boss's ideas. Prepare reports covering several prominent options. Use the one the boss favors.
- Never let on when they get to you.
- Try to discover what others are doing. Take credit for their successes or help them fail.
- Always look out for old number one.
- Never give emotional support; it's a sign of weakness.
- It's not too hard to discover the failings of others. Harp on them.

Trying to get work done in such a climate can be strenuous indeed. Since few people are consciously aware of their motives, an early goal of a development program is to bring motives to the surface and make them visible. Freeing workers from destructive politics and games creates enthusiasm and releases great amounts of energy for problem solving.

One might suppose that in a business organization there would be high clarity on purpose and unit goals. In reality, much confusion can occur. When organizational members are working at cross-purposes, it is important to assist them in clarifying their purpose and goals. When misunderstanding is reduced, work efforts become more coherent and productive.

3. *Groupthink erodes members' integrity.* Since the days when rulers lopped off the heads of those bearing bad news, it has been clear that there are powerful forces working against social candor. In an old-style organization, powerful forces work to nullify critical thinking and moral judgment. Concerned about survival, concurrence, and approval, old-style managers go down with things they wouldn't tolerate if faced alone. They devise hidden agendas to preserve solidarity at the expense of moral and ethical considerations.*

4. *Games replace authentic encounters.* In games, words and behavior conflict. The real communication is in the behavior, and someone is put on, put off, or put down. Games always wreck relationships, foster cynicism, and corrode the group process. Old-style organizations are fertile soil for game players. They offer a good opportunity to study the entire repertoire of business games, especially "Gotcha," "Blemish," "Ain't It Awful," and "If It Weren't for Them" (see Chapter 10). When games are *de rigueur,* no one will take the risk of owning

* See Dudley Bennett, *TA and the Manager* (New York: AMACOM, 1976). Chapter 6 expands this phenomenon.

up for fear of ridicule or embarrassment. There is a downward spiral in group process until behavior is highly constricted, defensive, and ritualized. Trust is nonexistent in such organizations. When process is diminished, communication breaks down and rumor is rampant. Change is resistant at all levels, thinking is inhibited and narrow, and heaps of energy go into "covering your ass."

Group process is the way things are done in an organization. It is the total pattern of accepted beliefs, customs, opinions, allowable feelings, and behavior. Sometimes called culture or style, it is the map of the social territory you must learn to read if you are going to get along. Usually unseen, it powerfully controls members' behavior. It defines the typical or acceptable social transaction and is the source of how members value themselves. Group process supplies answers to questions like these: "What is the best way to do a job?" "What is an acceptable level of accomplishment?" "How should managers and workers relate?" "What is the value of education?"

5. *Problem-solving techniques are weak.* Underutilizing member resources plus moving problems around weakens decision making and problem solving. Not seeing problems (and hence not having to take responsibility) and discussing problems at great length are old-style maladies. "There's no problem so big I can't overlook it," the bureaucrat crows. At all levels workers go to great pains not to be visible, not to have opinions, and not to care about results. The goal of a development program is to create space for workers to see and solve problems and to tell the truth.

NEW-STYLE SKILLS

What are the characteristics of a new-style organization that is able to fashion powerful responses to the shifting marketplace? A new-style company is democratic and familial. It is visualized as a group of equals in a circle. Among them, leadership shifts to those whose particular competence at the moment gives them precedence. Leadership is based more on competence than on status. The mode of the new-style organization is knowledge, and the mechanism is collaboration. Power flows from the bottom up. Models are high-technology companies that reward creativity, risk taking, team playing, and hard work.

Old-style systems avoided feelings. New-style systems enable people to be involved with the full range of their personalities. Old style denied conflict and repressed fight. It meant constriction of information flow and management by secrecy. New style means an openness that builds trust throughout the organization. Old style was win-lose. New style is win-win.

The key skill necessary for managers in the technological age is ability to make decisions collaboratively. This involves building trust, supporting intimacy, and sharing responsibility in problem solving. In the old system, neighboring workers were viewed as competitors rather than as resources for joint problem solving. In the new system, emphasis is placed on building trust and collaborating in solving problems. The outcome of this is a reduction of ritual management.

How many times have you sat in a room where the anger hung heavy in the air and everyone smiled? How many times have you sat in a room where, if you didn't know better, you might think that what people were talking about was the subject under discussion? How many times have you sat in a room where leadership was obviously on a deadend course and everyone went along? How many times have you sat in a room where you were confident that what people were saying was not what they really believed? Such scenes are commonplace in a system based on fear and obedience. Thoughtful workers are tired of this kind of unproductive, ritualistic, status-seeking behavior.

New-style collaboration is not a democratic gesture; nor is it a technique. The resources we seek for the difficult challenges of the future lie inside the workers themselves—all workers. It is part of their elegance, even when they don't know it. This is not a belief. It is not a moral or ethical position. It is simply what's so. If we operated only on the technique level, the development program wouldn't work. It's because at some level workers understand their own elegance that new style can have spectacular success.

Another skill of the new-style manager is upward influence. In old-style companies, this idea was so unusual it was called rebellion. Workers looked upward for guidance and blamed others for failure, blind to their own responsibility for the larger system. Internal restraints against being "uppity," seeing oneself as "better than others," and acting above one's "position and station" make it difficult for people to accept responsibility for larger systems and higher authority.

Often, criticism of higher levels is based on knowledge of lower levels only. The differences between the levels of a company are often so great that such criticism has no meaning. Discussion of a problem needs to occur on the level the problem exists. The best salesman on the force may not understand the problems of being a sales manager. Open discussion should not stop. Upward influence in organizations, often from younger workers, is an important dynamic in new-style companies. Such influence must be suited to the problem. This is the test for any posited solution. The solution must solve the problem as it is. To solve a problem as it isn't is failure guaranteed.

Our republican form of government creates institutions wherein the influence of the populace can be meaningfully expressed. The executive, legislative, and judicial branches are structured to reflect and be responsive at all levels to the will of the people. Upward influence will be an increasingly important skill as the country faces the complex problems of the future. As we search for dynamic ways to influence our government on particular issues, a collective mind will be created that is larger than the sum of its parts. It is through a sense of awareness shared by a majority around a problem that power flows into the larger system.

A central new-style skill is that of giving and receiving helpful help. Problems arise on both sides of the helping equation—that is, in both giving and receiving. We describe this awkwardly as the consultant–client relationship. The chief rule for giving help, or being a consultant, is that what you offer must seem like help to the recipient. Anything else is "helping the hell out of someone." A good consultant strengthens the recipient's ability to meet, define, and solve problems. Solving problems for others and building other forms of dependency is not good help.

Asking for help, or being a client, involves being realistic about one's needs and not surrendering one's power in the situation. Some managers refuse assistance for fear that they will appear weak or imperfect. In old-style systems, one never asked for help. Thoughtful managers today refuse to buy that macho act. They are no longer willing to operate in a way that insists they act as if they were omnicompetent. Advanced technology makes such a position ludicrous.

Team building, another skill necessary in contemporary organizations, is a well-developed piece of technology. It assumes a continual expansion of subordinate participation, self-direction, and self-control in decision making. The strategy is to make company problems, group process, member behavior, and motivation available to workers at all levels. This is done through a variety of activities which we will examine in later chapters. The creative resource of a company is its people, who are seldom offered the opportunity to perform anywhere near their capabilities. When given the opportunity, workers will exercise responsible self-direction. They will grow.

Temporary systems are going to play an increasingly important role in today's complex urban society. People are going to have to come together, get the garbage out of their relationships, accomplish agreed-upon goals, and split. They are going to have to do this or get run over with problems.

Team building is a problem-solving strategy. It begins and ends there. It also has a training component—to help members bring process and behavior under management. The mechanism of team building is the development of workers while they advance toward resolution of daily business problems. Team building is especially useful for start-up and project teams. It is also valuable when new members arrive and when the company is faced with a crisis. All teams, including those that are winners, find it useful to go through the process as least once a year.

In an old-style organization "most people" agreed that nice guys don't fight. This usually worked out to mean nice guys fight dirty. There is nothing in new-style management that disallows passionate disagreement. Reasonable people disagree. Indeed, often it is useful if they do so wholeheartedly. Some issues are worthy of it. They demand powerful application of our intelligence, passions, and values. Nothing in new style suggests managers should be less powerful than they are. We hold this standard to fight: Is it productive? Organizations need to differentiate between destructive and constructive fight, for which the nomenclature is usually "clean" and "dirty." At the process level the task is to make passive aggression active and covert fight overt. In general, dirty fight attacks opponents on qualities they can't change and weakens them so they cannot continue the struggle. If you win too big and weaken your opponent's ability to fight, he will reach for a bigger stick. It is not useful to escalate. The issue is not what the fighter intends but what's happening to the opponent.

Win or lose, everyone who has been in a clean fight has experienced coming away feeling OK. People are not pleased by a loss, but they feel that they have struggled well, that issues have been clarified, and that they will be able to confront the issue on another day. Elements of a clean fight include openness, a focus on issues and on the here and now, verbal clarity, specificity, and directness. Confronting in the open rather than settling old scores contributes to successful fight. So do focusing on issues instead of people, being clear about areas of disagreement, and confronting directly rather than tangentially. More difficult for many than the fight itself is the guilt they experience afterward. Learning how to fight successfully and without guilt is a major gain for new-style workers.

Just as neighboring workers do not see themselves as resources to each others' problems, so neighboring organizations filled with competent people view the same problems silently unaware of each other. Creating an interface between up- and downstream organizations is a powerful new-style skill. Some of the most successful work done in new-style programs has been to replace pro forma single-face relationships between organizations with in-depth, issue-focused, multiple relationships. The interface is structured by team-building both organizations separately around the issues that relate them to each other. From these sessions an agenda is created for the joint meeting. Both teams come together to solve their problems. Process issues include how to give helpful help and build a social contract. Behavior issues usually include interrupting games and overcoming resistance. The results have sometimes been astonishing.

The ability to complete relationships is another new-style skill. On the process level, this has to do with completing contracts fully and bringing closure to organizational relationships. When interpersonal relationships are incomplete, with things left unsaid and issues unresolved, the social fabric is damaged. When organizations are unwilling to bring about closure in their relationships, they lose power. Accepting poor quality from vendors, allowing subordinates to promise more than they can deliver, and not confronting problems are circuits left unclosed. Confronting a problem means bringing it to the surface, dealing with it, and resolving it. Powerful teams do not leave issues unresolved. They work constantly toward closure.

There is no ideal way to run a company. The style that best gets the job done is the "right one." A large Eastern banking institution has a "check bashing" department that each morning faces the task of keypunching close to 100,000 checks. At present, optical scanners are not economically feasible for the company. The bank hires dozens of keypunch operators who are capable of doing a dull, monotonous job over long periods of time with low levels of boredom and error.

There isn't a whole lot you can do to enrich such a job. A balance must be maintained. If you push to increase operator production, errors will increase—errors that can be embarrassing and difficult to correct. Hygiene can be improved, and there is motivational potential in the areas of recognition, promotion, and team bonuses. However, keypunching remains a monotonous job. The bank is committed to automating it at the earliest possible moment. In the meantime, its contract with employees runs like this:

> We want to hire people who can do a dull, monotonous job over long periods of time relatively error-free and with low levels of boredom. We will pay you money to do this. It is not expected that you like us or that we like you, but only that you do the job with relatively few errors.

I have no quarrel with this contract—though I do believe there is no job that can't be enriched. Someone within the bank described managers in the keypunch area as definitely old style. Other parts of the organization find new style much more congenial and productive. Management seeks to automate routine work as soon as the technology is in place and is proven cost-effective.

Bank officials are fully aware they preside over a multifaceted organization composed of both old and new style. They remain clear about their goals. They seek to develop employees and at the same time accomplish the organization's mission. Their task is not simple, but then challenges of the marketplace are not getting simpler either. Companies are not usually old style or new style. In the most rigid organization there will be productive individuals who enjoy the full cooperation and trust of subordinates.

Old style is not wrong. It made America a great industrial nation, accomplished prodigious feats during World War II, and made possible our great venture to the moon. But the age of technology demands behavior not possible under old style. Creativity, provisional attempts, willingness to make mistakes, flexibility, high-speed problem solving, accelerating change, and handling vast fact patterns—these things topdown systems simply cannot deliver. Old-style managers tend to face problems by trundling out the old saws: "It's always worked this way before; we must be doing something right." "When you've got success going, don't monkey with it." "Let others take risks; I prefer the tried and true." Of all companies listed in the *Fortune* 100 in 1938, fully 80 percent are no longer on the list and many of them no longer exist. Change evidently proved a challenge too severe.

The task today is to equip organizations to identify and manage their own process in the direction they wish to go. This is a fully rational procedure. The movement is from not knowing to knowing, from reacting to planning, from business as usual to the most productive way, from old style to new style.

2

Structure and Function of Behavior

Our insides and outsides are in synchronization. They work together. If you look carefully at a person's outside—given a sound understanding of Transactional Analysis—you will know what's going on inside. To put it another way, a person's state comprises a specific state of consciousness along with its related patterns of behavior.

Human behavior is very regular. "Mostpeople," to use e e cummings' coinage, believe every action is discrete, separate, individual, subject only to the moment. They may see acts of behavior as the consequence of character, will power, sinfulness, or other unverified constructs. In fact, behavior is the consequence of adequate cause, largely social. It is because of these regularities that a science of human behavior is possible. Science is based on the regularity of nature. What we say about ego states we believe to be true any time, any place, anywhere in the past and the future. Our findings are not culture bound. While we know very little of the totality we suspect, we believe our assumptions and procedures are sound. What we do know is that others have found knowledge of behavior and process life-giving.

Another way of saying the same thing: An ego state is a set

of coherent feelings plus related behaviors. Feelings are in sync with bodily states. Frustration, anger, confusion, and hostility operate in tandem with a harmonious display of total system behavior. In anger, fists and teeth clench, heartbeat increases, blood lactate levels rise, adrenalin appears, and muscles go taut for fight or flight. Alternatively in the state of quietude, people experience clear perception, a sense of peace or wholeness, and relaxation. This state exactly reverses all the bodily tension signs that appear during fight mobilization.

Another way of defining ego states is to see them as experienced reality of bodily and mental states that have historically derived contents. All ego states are rooted in the individual's maturation process. Doing (in the automatic sense), thinking, and feeling are all derived from the sum total of life experiences. More precisely, they proceed out of infant experiences, developing until such time and in the event that the maturation process is stopped. When we say people are "stuck," we mean their ego state growth is arrested. In this position they are no longer open to new data and experiences but are able to respond only with stored materials of former age levels.

A large proportion of human behavior, then, is a reenactment of the past. Yet most people believe their behavior and consciousness are responses to the immediate environment. Because of its imminence and vividness, behavior seems to be here and now. Its compelling quality hides the fact that it is a restimulation of very old ego states, replayed for the umpteenth time with all their original intensity. This realization is a significant gain for those who have undertaken behavior training. From it people can begin to free themselves from archaic controls, take charge of their lives, and achieve benefits available to them only in present time.

There is a difference between memory and reliving. Reliving is holistic, involving feelings, ideas, details, and interpretations recalled from the past. Such behavior can be distinguished from present-time behavior that is responsive to immediate conditions. Living in present time gives the individual power to transform his or her life daily. It expands a person's sense of aliveness and enhances mental and physical health. Memory is the awareness of this process. Recall involves the total personality and engages far more than conscious retrieval, which we call memory. Past ego states can be spontaneously reactivated in a normal waking state or can be vitalized by electrical or pharmacological stimuli, dreams, or trance induction.

One or more ego states can be activated at the same time to occupy consciousness and yet remain discrete entities. One or two may be dominant, diminished, or excluded. Personality is a dynamic system in which all permutations imaginable happen from time to time. The basic TA model of personality is described below. The nomenclature relates to the origin of each state and of course conceals far more than it reveals. Each ego state is examined more fully later.

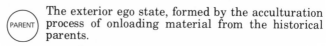

The exterior ego state, formed by the acculturation process of onloading material from the historical parents.

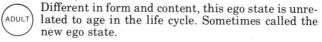

Different in form and content, this ego state is unrelated to age in the life cycle. Sometimes called the new ego state.

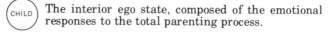

The interior ego state, composed of the emotional responses to the total parenting process.

Each ego state functions in a different way, responds to different stimuli, records a particular content, and perceives the environment according to its functioning. The goal of behavior training in a program of organizational development is to create more options for employees and expand their control of the three states. They learn to manage behavior like any business problem. They discover their ego state structures, separate them, strengthen or weaken boundaries, and put the Adult in control. This leads into transactional, script, and games analysis whereby they learn to control their own and indirectly others' wasteful manipulations. In the vernacular: "They get to get off their acts." They can stop their magic shows. By reducing unconsciousness, they expand their areas of social control.

PARENT EGO STATE

The Parent is that part of us that controls our behavior when we are on automatic. It is a huge storehouse of computer programs on how to do the things we do daily without thinking about them:

Driving a car.
Getting dressed.
Eating dinner.
Giving a party.
Talking to superiors.
Shopping for food.
Getting through the day.

The same apparatus operates with more complex matters:

Making love.
Taking out tonsils.
Building a house.
Programming a computer.
Worshipping God.
Selling automobiles.
Conducting class.

This material is welded powerfully into the personality at the youngest age by the various parental strategies that trade affection and support for obedience. In an entire lifetime we may receive no more compelling communication directed at us than the peremptory "dos" and "don'ts" from those omnipotent beings. It is no wonder the young child internalizes parental "oughts" and "musts" when delivered with absolute force from those gigantic people, who to the child's eyes are 15 feet tall and the source of all blessing. Not only do parents give biological life, they also define for us success, joy, pride, shame, and failure. They define and implant in us those things their parents believed to be true at a time when we have neither operable intelligence to understand nor the will to resist.

Parenting establishes within us the need to adorn ourselves with the protective coloring of our group. Beliefs, behavior, style of dress, attitudes, and positions are assumed from the environing social system. We feel comfortable and secure with this sense of membership or belonging with those of the same feather. These are exceedingly strong controls. The need to be "right," to be "on target," to belong, operates intensely in most of us, with much more force than we are aware. Deviance from social norms sets off a "tilt mechanism" in our heads and drives us back in line. It takes determination to reparent ourselves. It takes insight to value the self and see the usefulness of our contribution to social life in being only ourselves. We have to overcome that most powerful of human emotions—embarrassment. Social sanctions against deviance include coolness, exhortations to change, and, all else failing, exclusion. This pressure to conform is a great threat to healthy social functioning. Better risk rebellion. Resistance creates energy and is a source of vitality—the enemy of mediocrity and banality.

Parent material is implanted with great force. It is held with tenacious conviction. When such material is restimulated, people go into their acts and say the words and put on the display that always go with the topic. This is one of the first clues to Parent managers. They say the same things repeatedly. When you ask them a question on a topic they hold in the Parent, they go into their act. If you do not interfere when they get to the end, they'll go back to the beginning and start again. Like a broken record, they'll keep replaying until you stop them. The chief characteristic of the operant Parent is its inability to take in new data unless it fits what's already implanted. Parent managers are closed, fixed, set, "stoppered." In short, they're unconscious.

The value of the Parent is its ability to take over functioning in difficult or perilous situations. It is a superb time-saving mechanism for the mind. You simply don't have to think about everything you do. It would be a hopeless situation if everything you did required thought. Many things can be done effectively on automatic. Parent also has the built-in safety device of a quick-firing mechanism. Like an electrode it will cause you to react when immediate danger threatens and there is insufficient time to consider alternatives. This quick-firing mechanism, if it has a hair trigger, can be a source of great pain. If you ever found yourself riding a horse at full gallop and wondered how you got there, look to your Parent ego state quick-firing mechanism.

Parent is the self as institution. It is the self apart from or over against the changes and vicissitudes of life. It is our "positionality" when we confront the important things in our lives—work, politics, sex, and self. Since the content is onloaded into the personality like cargo onto a truck, the total load may be out of balance and really make no sense. Parent managers give themselves away when they say things that are mutually exclusive: "Now I want all of you to feel free to speak your mind. However, as you know, there are some subjects it makes no sense to talk about." The content of the Parent is unmediated—that is, it has not been tested by reasoned discussion. It is held in the personality without thinking. It then becomes our act. It's simply what we do when we are confronted with certain topics, problems, and situations.

The operation of the Parent ego state explains one of the most puzzling aspects of human behavior—the failure to learn.

Since the Parent is closed down, complete, and "right" just as it is, new experiences have no influence. They roll off us like water off a duck's back. It is painful to ask someone who has just been through an important experience what he or she learned and draw only a blank stare. It's depressing to realize a country can fight a war and have internalized no clear meanings or useful principles from the experience. Admittedly, clear meanings are hard to come by. That should not dissuade us from the task. "Those who cannot remember the past," as Santayana said, "are condemned to repeat it."

Werner Erhard, founder of est, includes a story called "The Rat and Cheese" in his training program. The rat, it is reported, found the cheese after exploring the end of the fourth tunnel. One day the cheese was missing from its usual place and, though apprehensive, the rat began exploring again. *Voilà,* it found the biggest and best hunk of cheese ever at the end of another tunnel. The est story continues: "Now, up to a point, a human being will behave exactly like a rat. The difference is that eventually the rat will stop going down the fourth tunnel and will begin to look down other tunnels. The human being may go down the fourth tunnel forever.... Rats know only from cheese; humans want to be in the 'right' tunnel."

Our act doesn't have to make sense. It's just our act. It doesn't have to reflect life, decent thought, or even ourselves. It's just the way we do it. Material contained in the Parent will often be contradictory, inconsistent, and confusing. Grandparents and parents did not bother to think carefully, organize, focus, or challenge belief systems. They just believed them. Education was indoctrination, not learning. And we parent in the same way. It is this arbitrary, absolute, unthinking quality of Parent behavior that colors it crazy. It is also the source of the ironic humor: "If you believe something, it's a lie."

The effectiveness of an individual in later life is in part a function of what material was programmed into his or her

Parent, or how the person was scripted. Fortunate is the person who was programmed with the following:

Truth will out.
All deserve justice.
Love is stronger than hate.
Hard work is the source of human dignity.
Teamwork is the most effective way.
Women (men) are a wonderful alternative.
Life is a mysterious blessing.

Those in whom these notions are implanted face life one up. They are preset for success. Their self-fulfilling prophecy gives them health. They know nothing succeeds like success. The arbitrariness of the Parent works in their favor. Despite conditions to the contrary, they go on believing in human potential and making lemonade out of their lemons. Such people uplift us all.

Others, unfortunately, are enjoined with somewhat less sanguine injunctions:

Never give a sucker an even break.
Never trust anyone.
Attack is the best defense.
Never lose control.
Strength is the only security.
That sort is no good.
Our kind would never cry.
Eggheads know nothing.

Programmed with material of this caliber and closed to new ideas, the Parent-dominant individual survives primarily by two garden-variety strategies: denial and projection. They are so familiar to us that we often don't recognize them. Whatever doesn't fit a person's programming just doesn't exist. If the person can't deny its existence, he or she will deny its relevance or attack its rightness. For the Parent, if it doesn't fit, it is either wrong or irrelevant. Something has meaning only if the Parent grants it. It doesn't have meaning simply by its existence.

The second way the closed mind works is by projection. Parent types take their belief system and project it onto the world. By remaking the world in their own image, they can speak to and transact with it. The world is only what they see. By diminishing, excluding, and distorting, they make reality over to fit their preconceptions. They live inside their heads, or at least in a world they create with their heads. It's more comfortable that way and takes a lot less energy. This is a fundamental dynamic that workers must be trained to resist if we are to create healthy companies. "Perception is often 90 percent projection," we constantly remind ourselves.

The Parent is composed of material from the parents and grandparents. When the Parent is restimulated, people are being their own historical parents again. The Parent lives on in the persona of the offspring. Words, gestures, voice tones, and content will duplicate the parents. If we were able to know both the person and the parents, the comparison would be surprising. Saying the Parent ego state is active means our parent is talking now. There is also an internal or covert expression of the parent. When behavior is under the control of the internalized parent, we are operating in compliance with parental desires. Our historical parents may be dead, but we continue to respond to their programming. Rather than being autonomous and self-directed, we are compliant and obedient to the internal voice in our head. This explains people who move through social situations seemingly oblivious to external stimuli, people whose responses appear lifeless and sterile. Their strings are being pulled by a surrogate inside them.

The Parent ego state is divided into two large bodies of activities: nurturing and punishing. In the programming of males the concept of dominance and control looms large. Young men are scripted:

Be the best.
Never be "yellow."
Don't tread on me.
No one attacks me with impunity.
Physical combat is glorious (the John Wayne syndrome).
Guns are symbols of manhood.
Never give in.

Attack comprises a significant portion of most Parent behavior. Quick, automatic judgments delivered with scorn and condescension are characteristic. Tone of voice is accusing and demanding, often shrill and loud. Facial expressions include rolling the eyes upward, stern gaze, pursed lips, jutting chin, and an overall look of disapproval. Posture may be bent forward behind pointing index finger, or it may be a soldiering stance with thrust-back shoulders, expanded chest, and puffed-up appearance. Vocabulary includes purple words like "should," "ought," "must," and "never." The major technique is putting others in the wrong. The person seems to be saying: "Except for you, everything would be all right."

The Punishing Parent is intimidating. One can easily jump to the conclusion such demeanor must cloak knowledge and competence. Often quite the opposite is true. Judgments may be based on infant data. The question a lurking Adult will ask: "I hear your conviction. Let's discuss the content of the problem before us." Typically, this will reveal a rigid personality that has limited itself, is unwilling to take part in give-and-take, and is unable to learn.

There is another side to the Parent. When someone falls and you reach quickly to help, that is the Nurturing Parent. Any automatic behavior that demonstrates support and concern falls here. Observation suggests this is a smaller part. Nurturing Parent is exhibited in behavior that suggests protection, support, and concern. Gestures include shielding, supporting, lifting, protecting, and hugging. Bonding gestures include the shared glance, handshake, wink, pat on the back, and arm around the shoulder. The face expresses openness, concern, warmth, and happiness, accompanied by a comforting and caring voice.

The quality of a person's parenting has a compelling influence on his or her later successes and failures. One of the goals of organizational development is to create a Nurturing Parent environment in which workers can be released from their fixations and begin growing again. Growing is stretching. Learning is demanding. The goal of a development program is to create an environment in which employees can ask for and get the tools they need to return to the credit side of the ledger. Acceptance and encouragement are the soil of growth. If we are not nurtured, we cannot grow, cannot make it up the steep grade. The company can become the neo-parent that makes growth possible. Management can make its power available to everyone so that employees, if they desire, can expand their control over the work process. When employees take charge of process and behavior, they develop new and rationally held Parent positions. The process is called reparenting.

CHILD EGO STATE

To the degree that we are patterned and to the degree that our thinking follows the laws of logic, we are like everyone else. That which is only us and no one else is that historically derived set of feelings and related behaviors that compose our affective (emotional) responses to life. This is our Child ego state. It is uniquely us. It is the most powerful and consequently, we judge, the most important of all our ego states.

Observation indicates that it is the most underutilized ego state among workers.

Most people would agree that they first think about what they are going to do and then do it. The consequence of their action, they believe, is feelings. Using that theory to understand behavior is a hopeless task. Feelings come first, then action, then explanations of the action. Feelings stimulate behavior, after which we attempt to make sense out of the behavior, often referring to some external agency. "He made me mad." "I did what I was told." Such explanations often sound phony. That is why they are called "think about" and "talk about." To understand worker behavior, we have to understand feelings, where they come from, their expression, and their consequences.

All events in our lives—those we were paying attention to—are recorded indelibly in our storage banks and can be recalled. Recall is not the same as memory. Total recall includes feelings, ideas, interpretations, and attitudes. The content of the Child is historical people and genuine events. Personality, like a house, is built from the foundation up. Most of our attitudes and behaviors were set in infancy. By the age of three, children have experienced the entire range of human emotions. The rest of their emotional lives is at best a refinement and reinforcement of those earliest years. The Child's feelings and behaviors record the response to what the individual heard, felt, saw, and understood in the earliest years. It contains historical moments of a particular time in the person's development.

Our basic feeling position toward life—the emotional lens through which we look out on the world—was developed before we were rational beings. We developed our emotional mind set before we could think. In response to our parenting, we couldn't make comparative judgments, put off drawing conclusions, and seek clarifying help. All usual rational operations were not available to us. They hadn't arrived yet. All we could do was experience life; we could only begin recording our history of feelings. The feelings we experience today are replays of old tapes. They are not fresh and unique, as their immediacy and potency might suggest.

The emotions we experience today are the same emotions we experienced in childhood. This leads to an explanation of a number of perplexing things about behavior. Others do not cause our feelings, as many suppose. At best they are the occasion. Mistakenly a person says, "George makes me mad." "George," we reply, "is being George and what you make out of that is anger." Others, witnessing the same behavior, feel many different things: sympathy, chagrin, confusion, even pleasure. People cause their own feelings. They can create any feeling they desire by initiating the related behavior. Learning to take responsibility for your own behavior means developing the ability to feel what you want to feel. "Don't be angry when you're angry," we counsel. "Be angry only when you want to be angry. Don't put yourself under another's control. Don't give away your power. Keep your feeling behavior under your own management." Developing your options means, in part, being able to energize your Child ego state with feelings appropriate to the situation confronting you.

When we say feelings are not rational, we mean they may not be responsive to circumstances of the immediate environment. Historically derived, they may as yet not be under effective Adult control. All behavior makes sense in terms of the circumstances of your upbringing. You would understand it if you could see how it was fashioned to cope with your childhood experiences. Rooted in the past, behavior may be inappropriate to present realities. Such behavior may be described as unconscious and, if extravagant or odd, as "crazy." To say that behavior is irrational does not mean it does not have adequate cause that can be understood. When people cause themselves to fail or to be dissatisfied, they are, in fact, responding as best they know how. That is, they are making the best choice available to them, given their parenting and historical development.

When we say behavior is crazy, we mean it is counterproductive in present time, although it may be perfectly consistent with the individual's background. People can be empowered to strengthen their Adult controls and replace crazy behavior with behavior that is more productive.

When a person's response is excessive and not related to the stimulus, it usually means that a sensitive area has been touched. Such a sensitive area, laden with explosive material (fear, hurt, frustration), is caused by continuously "packing in" bad feelings and not dealing with them. Feelings, if expressed, deplete. Emotions, if surfaced, disappear. It is one of the marvelous things about human beings. Life is naturally frustrating. There is no way to escape anger. If anger is denied or ignored, it is daily packed in, continually loading the personality. It will be expressed one way or another. There are many indirect forms of anger. Phobias, fantasies, sickness, suicide at various speeds, fanaticism, rage at subordinates, crime, and hard work can all at times be expressions of anger. When anger, under Adult control, is immediately and appropriately expressed, the individual is healthier. If the individual continually packs anger in, it becomes a suppurating wound that, when the person's "button is pressed," may explode into bizarre behavior.

Another reason the Child ego state is most important is because, sequentially considered, it is the first activated. Ego state firing order is usually Child-Parent-Adult: feeling, acting, thinking. Because the sequence happens so quickly, a restimulation of past feelings may take place, surface to cause behavior, and disappear again before we become aware of it. Behavior training teaches us to become sensitive to these "flicker" stimulations of the Child. When we discover them, we can track down where we are coming from and then fashion responses that are more suitable to our needs and goals.

The Child ego state is referred to as the "little boy" or "little girl" within us, since it perceives life as it did when we were infants. It has lived with the extremes of dependency and helplessness. The myth of a happy childhood probably needs shattering, along with that of Santa Claus. All of us have a handicapped little person inside who has suffered simply because of radical dependency, fear, rage, and guilt. Most people come out of this with a basic Not OK position. They are constantly working uphill to achieve a sense of OK.

Because of this negative bias toward life and the seeming unavailability of happiness, people behave in ways congruent with their predisposition. Fearful people often bully. Cynical people often scheme. Worried people often retreat. Such behavior evokes the response from others that we were predisposed to believe was there in the first place. By proving what we said was true, we defeat ourselves again. We're caught in a spiral movement downward. With this imbalance, one negative discount wipes out five positive strokes. In other words, one "you idiot" wipes out five "atta boys."

People need strokes as much as they need vitamins. Because they start from a deficiency (Not OK) position and because work life is often debilitating, most workers survive in a stroke-starved economy. Stroke deprivation is the source of much organizational dysfunction. An important rule is: If you want to restore yourself, allow your Child to play. Play, that is, as you played as an infant, not as grownups play. Such restoration includes playing in water, stroking animals, walking in the woods, and touching your partner. People who give themselves such strokes give themselves strength. To heal others, support their Child. The more dysfunctional the individual, the more stroke-starved his or her child.

People are responsible for their own health. We are all responsible for ensuring that we get enough of the kinds of strokes that are important to us and that keep our energy up. Strokes to the Parent support our ancestry, national and military history, value system, and the like. Strokes to the Adult involve recognition of our ability to think clearly and accurately. Strokes to the Child please our sense of self. Some of the most successful people in business are those who are best able to give accurate and genuine strokes.

The little person inside us who needs support and caring is called the Natural Child. Another part of this ego state is composed of all the gimmicks, rackets, games, and scripts our Child learned as necessary to survival. This is our Adapted Child. When someone tells us that we'd feel proud if we had a Cadillac and we buy a Cadillac and feel proud—that's being adapted. In the Army we were taught that we'd feel like soldiers and members of the fighting team if our brass buckles and leather boots shone during Saturday morning inspection. They did and we did. If you think a woman dressed like a rabbit is sexy, you will recognize your Adapted Child.

Unfortunately, human development usually means systematic growth of the Adapted Child at the expense of the Natural Child. There is a consequent loss of vital, direct expression of feelings. In its place come synthetic attractions to things and distractions from the authentic self. When people act out tantrums, we say their Child is rebellious. When they are tired and out of sorts, their Child is distracted.

A third distinction is sometimes made in the Child ego state. Pointing to its manipulative, intuitive, and creative abilities, some refer to the Little Professor. He has "smarts." With almost the quality of a magician, he turns events to his own ends. He looks like he's scheming, but he's not thinking. He's the prototypical Adult. The Little Professor likes new ideas, is charming, and is proficient at getting his way.

ADULT EGO STATE

The Adult ego state is of a different type and function from the other two. Depending on how much it is used, it can be relatively strong or weak. It is the one ego state that is not historically derived. It can function only in the here and now. After about five years it is totally there and ready to operate perfectly. Because the radio is not turned on doesn't mean it is broken. While potentially the Adult is the strongest, both Parent and Child always attempt to usurp control. When their attempts at seizing control are partially effective, we say the Adult is contaminated. A Parent-contaminated Adult has trouble separating what it believes from what is objectively true. Prejudice is a form of Parent contamination. A Child-contaminated Adult cannot clearly distinguish feelings from thinking. Fantasy is a form of Child contamination.

The Adult is the only ego state that can function in present time. When it asserts authority over the Parent and Child, we say the Adult has executive over the personality. When the Adult is energized, it can emancipate itself from boundary incursions of the other two. The task is to clear boundaries, not to decommission the other two. People need all three to function effectively. When the Adult has executive, it reduces internal dissonance by organizing the input from the other two, clarifying their communication, and deciding on the most effective course to pursue.

When facing a problem, the Adult asks and receives answers to three sets of questions:

1. What does my Parent have to say about this issue? What values, judgments, and opinions are recorded there? How strongly does the Parent feel on this topic, and are these feelings appropriate? Does this position have an objective base? Does the position have ethical content?
2. What does my Child feel about the issue? Is the feeling strongly motivated in one direction? What is the founda-

tion for this feeling or lack of feeling? Can my Child be trusted in this area, and what were my past results? What are the sources of my motivation? What would be the consequences of giving my Child head in this matter?

3. What does my Adult know to be objectively true about this matter, shorn of opinions and feelings? What can be known or found out about this matter in my environment? What do the records show? How compelling is the proof? What are the opinions of experts?

By separating the ego states and examining their content individually, we make our thinking more potent. What was before a confusing welter of conflicting advice and desires now becomes a clear printout of communication. Strengthening this process makes us more intelligent.

The Adult has three functions that are not found in the other ego states. First, the Adult can take in new data and sort it in a variety of ways according to content. Second, stored material can be retrieved from memory, organized, and compared with other data both inside and outside the system. Third, alternative courses for the future can be plotted, and the probabilities of various alternatives can be estimated. All these are a basis for action. The Adult as executive of the personality is the model for a worker's self-development program. Such a program might have a variety of goals, including decontaminating and strengthening the Adult, reparenting (up-parenting) the self along more realistic lines, and developing a rational ethic. Discharging Child contaminate and strengthening and possibly enlarging affect structure are also part of sensitizing the whole personality.

The concept of self needs clarification. We say an individual is unconscious if his Parent or Child has control and his Adult is either temporarily decommissioned or excluded. Under this condition the energy in the Parent or Child is uncontrolled, unbound, or explosive. When the Parent or Child is cathectic—empowered with great energy—in the absence of the Adult, consequences for the individual cannot be sanguine. Early behavior training is dedicated to separating ego states (decontaminating) and empowering the Adult. By this process the person expands his or her choice of behavior. The person has free choice of which ego state behavior to use under specific conditions. The ego state energized by free choice is the "real self." When my Child is allowed to play in the sun and ocean with my Adult attentive nearby—that's my real self. Free choice is the precondition for discovery of the self.

Thus when the Adult is emancipated and in control, a person does not say "I'm mad as hell," but "My kid is mad as hell." Or the person may aver: "I'm tired of doing this job. And so I get to do the job tired." About the Parent, the person can own: "My Parent dislikes what you have done; you have offended its position; however, I will understand where you are coming from and deal with the Parent myself." In such a situation the individual may report more directly: "I'm angry with you; but that's my problem and I'll deal with it."

THE PAC OBSERVER'S RECORD

There are four ways of diagnosing which ego state energizes a person. Observation of all relevant behavior clues is primary. Behavior is far more revealing about what the actor is up to than most of us realize. You can use the PAC Observer's Record on the facing page to organize your observations of member behavior during a meeting. The record can be used to assist individuals in improving their competence and to aid the group in discussing process. (An audio recording will help in cross-checking.)

1. *Frequency count.* A tick mark is made next to the "S" symbol each time the individual initiates discussion with a question, statement, or opinion. A similar mark is made oppo-

PAC OBSERVER'S RECORD

NAME	FREQUENCY COUNT OF ENTRANCES S = Initiating R = Responding	LISTENING ACTIVITY — Listening — Hearing — Withdrawal	POSTURE, GESTURES, MANNERISMS, FACIAL EXPRESSIONS	KEY WORDS AND VOICE TONE PARENT : Sarcastic, disgusted, judgmental ADULT : Matter-of-fact, straightforward CHILD : Excited, fearful, sullen, rebellious
0010	P A C S R			
0020	P A C S R			
0030	P A C S R			
0040	P A C S R			

site the "R" each time he responds to others' initiatives or joins his comments to that of another. Frequency of contribution is one measure of leadership.

2. *Listening activity.* Listening can take place in all three ego states and has a dynamic effect on the speaker. Active listening is a positive stroke. "Withdrawal" is avoidance of contact, usually evidenced by a cessation of listening activity. It is debilitating to a speaker. "Hearing" is the preconscious auditory scanning of the social situation for suitable material to respond to. All of us do it without knowing it. We pick up and listen to things just long enough to ascertain their probable usefulness to us. "Listening" is an active enterprise. There is much large-muscle activity when members are alert, involved, and attentive.

3. *Posture and gestures.* Scrutiny of posture and mannerisms will tell a great deal about what is going on inside an individual. It is important to describe behavior rather than report such conclusions as the member is "bored" or "fatigued." Since all behavior counts, the more accurate and complete the observations, the easier to spot the operant ego state.

4. *Voice tone and vocabulary.* Probably more ego state information is revealed through voice tone, quality, emphasis, rate of speech, and word coloring than through any other behavior.

5. *PAC profile.* You should fill out the member profiles only after the meeting has ended. Decide what percentage of time you believe each person spent in each of the three ego states and fill in the appropriate box. The total will be larger than 100, since members often are in multiple states at the same time. It must be remembered that this profile represents behavior under a particular set of circumstances for a definite period of time. Generalizations from such limited data must be made with caution.

Social diagnosis, the second way of observing what motivates an individual, focuses on the consequences of behavior in a social setting and argues backward to the causal ego state. In subjective diagnosis, the third approach, the worker reports his own judgments and feelings. If this can be done with minimal distortion, it is the most direct way. Historical trackdown of the person's antecedents is the fourth method of diagnosis. Delving into a worker's past is not ordinarily a suitable business practice. Still, it is surprising how much people in the same organization know about each other's lives and backgrounds.

3

Self-Scoring Profiles of Organizational Characteristics

Managers may gain insight into the culture and typical behaviors of their organization by using the questionnaire in this chapter. It is a learning device, and the results should not be taken too seriously. Interpretation of the results and plans for remediation presume some knowledge of Transactional Analysis. Results are discussed at the end of the chapter.

The questionnaire was developed to help organizations describe the management culture or characteristic style used as they solve problems. Experience suggests organizations have a style that corresponds to and is consequent upon the major behavior descriptions used in Transactional Analysis—Parent (Punishing and Nurturing), Adult, and Child (Natural and Adaptive). From an organizational perspective we have identified these as Blaming (B), Benign Control (BC), Problem-solving (P-S), Spontaneous/Creative (S/C), and Distracting (D).

The historical development of an organizational culture has the following elements. There is domination of the emergent organization by a significant leader. People are selected in and out of the organization by the complementary nature of their ego states, games, and rackets. At some point the organization reaches critical mass, where the culture takes on a life of its own and begins to inbreed itself with appropriate organizational arrangements and devices. At this juncture a particular culture becomes normative and is accepted as "natural."

The fifty-five items on the scale are the key organizational variables to be considered when examining the health of the organization. The five vertical columns represent the five organizational systems described above. The cells of the matrix reveal the characteristic behavior of individuals within the system with regard to that variable.

The major organizational variables considered include:

Goal setting and ordering priorities (items 1–3)
Communications flow (items 4–15)
The decision-making process (items 16–22)
The control function (items 23–27)
Character of manager behavior (items 28–35)
Typical transactions (items 36–41)
Nature of motivational forces (items 42–48)
Development and training (items 49–51)
Performance appraisal and goals (items 52–55)

The questionnaire begins on the following page and continues through this chapter.

Below is a list (vertically) of 55 items that represent nine fundamental organizational variables. The relative integration and productivity of any organization can be judged by the assessment of these nine categories or organizational behavior. Within each item (horizontally) there are five ways members of an organization might behave. Our experiences suggest an organization will have one of these five "styles" as dominant, but may from time to time exhibit one or two of the alternate modes. This is not a test. There are no right or wrong answers. It is a diagnostic tool to assist managers to understand why their organization (unit) functions the way it does and what they can do about it.

Based on your experience, place a mark in each cell that best represents the frequency of that behavior in your organization. Use the following as a guide.

0 - Never occurs   1 - Rarely occurs   2 - Sometimes occurs   3 - Often occurs   4 - Usually occurs

1. GOAL SETTING

Agreement arises easily and quickly among those who share the same perspective. Intuition valued.	Little thought is given to goals. "Why question past success?"	Goals are set low to avoid expected resistance: they may or may not make sense in terms of present realities.	Goals are made by consensus among those related to the problem. Past and future considered.	Goals are set after reports and discussion by subordinates of the probabilities of alternative courses.
0 1 2 3 4	0 1 2 3 4	0 1 2 3 4	0 1 2 3 4	0 1 2 3 4

2. ACCEPTANCE OF ORDERS

Freely accepted. Immediate and direct response.	Overtly accepted but covertly resisted. Games: "Ain't it Awful" and "If it Weren't For Them I Could."	"Anything you say boss." Game: "Gee You're Wonderful..."	Accepted interdependence between individual and group. Disagreements are openly discussed.	Accepted with moderate amounts of resistance.
0 1 2 3 4	0 1 2 3 4	0 1 2 3 4	0 1 2 3 4	0 1 2 3 4

3. GOAL PERFORMANCE AT DIFFERENT LEVELS

High goals sought at all levels and met with enthusiasm and energy.	Senior individuals seek unrealistic goals with no awareness of subordinates' problems. Creates high resistance.	Productivity goals stressed by top and resisted at bottom.	All levels pursue high goals with junior levels sometimes pressing for higher goals than senior levels.	Continually pressing for higher goals among senior people. General acceptance at lower levels.
0 1 2 3 4	0 1 2 3 4	0 1 2 3 4	0 1 2 3 4	0 1 2 3 4

A.

S/C	B	D	P-S	BC

4. TIME SPENT ON THE PROBLEMS

	0	1	2	3	4
Shouts, threats, games, and politics substitute for problem-solving					

	0	1	2	3	4
Adult-Adult transactions between individuals and groups.					

	0	1	2	3	4
The discussion is hard to follow and conclusions are unclear. Lots of stroking.					

	0	1	2	3	4
Among senior members maintainance of good will and "going along" are stressed.					

	0	1	2	3	4
Withdrawals, pastimes, and rituals used to avoid the hard work of thinking.					

5. DISCUSSION OF INDIVIDUAL BEHAVIOR AND GROUP PROCESS

	0	1	2	3	4
Insistance on the status quo. Task, not people, is important.					

	0	1	2	3	4
Owning up to motivations, giving and receiving helpful feedback, makes each day a learning experience.					

	0	1	2	3	4
Excited by new insights and skills found in discussing process and others behavior.					

	0	1	2	3	4
Cautiously willing to try something new.					

	0	1	2	3	4
Fearful. Defensive. Uses insights to trap others.					

6. DIRECTION OF COMMUNICATION FLOW

Option	0	1	2	3	4
Downward with threats.					
In all directions openly.					
Whatever direction feels good.					
Downward with some horizontal.					
Any direction is defensive.					

7. WILLINGNESS OF TOP MANAGERS TO SHARE INFORMATION OPENLY WITH SUBORDINATES

Option	0	1	2	3	4
Management by secrecy and threat.					
Shares freely. Provides all information subordinates request or explains his refusal.					
Spontaneous information flows to people he likes.					
Provides information superior feels subordinates need to do their job.					
Information used for manipulative value.					

8. ACCEPTANCE AND TRUST OF TOPSIDE COMMUNICATIONS BY SUBORDINATES

Viewed with distrust and scrutinized for its political value.	Accepted along with openness to ask questions for clarification and enlargement.	Accepted at face value.	Accepted as necessary for the good of the organization.	Tolerated only and viewed with suspicion or indifference.
0 1 2 3 4	0 1 2 3 4	0 1 2 3 4	0 1 2 3 4	0 1 2 3 4

9. FREEDOM SUBORDINATES FEEL TO INITIATE "REAL" UPWARD INFORMATION FLOW

It would be viewed as defiance.	Considerable motivation and initiative taken based on ownership of company goals.	Willing to risk.	Only when requested and then highly filtered.	Own ideas not viewed as worthwile.
0 1 2 3 4	0 1 2 3 4	0 1 2 3 4	0 1 2 3 4	0 1 2 3 4

10. ORGANIZATION NORMS' SUPPORT OF REALISTIC UPWARD COMMUNICATION

Powerful forces tend to distort information and mislead superiors.

0	1	2	3	4

Organization rewards accurate, realistic, undistorted, communication.

0	1	2	3	4

"Talks off the top of his head." Idealistic.

0	1	2	3	4

Strong norms support "soldiering" and keeping bad news from topside.

0	1	2	3	4

Fear of Punishment causes reports to be continually "fudged"

0	1	2	3	4

11. REALISM AND ACCURACY OF UPWARD COMMUNICATIONS

Communication used politically.

0	1	2	3	4

Realistic, accurate, and here-and-now based.

0	1	2	3	4

Information may be exaggerated.

0	1	2	3	4

Boss is told what he wants to hear; other information is restricted, colored or cautiously given.

0	1	2	3	4

Unrealistic and inaccurate.

0	1	2	3	4

12. EASE OF HORIZONTAL COMMUNICATION FLOW

Low trust level is basis of games, hostility, and politics, replacing communication.

0	1	2	3	4

Freely and openly. People are given opportunities to work process and "discharge".

0	1	2	3	4

Often with humor and play.

0	1	2	3	4

Only among those on the "team".

0	1	2	3	4

Competitive feelings and defensive attitudes.

0	1	2	3	4

13. SOCIAL DISTANCE BETWEEN SUPERIORS AND SUBORDINATES

Great distance. Fear familiarity might reduce ones status and lessen control.

0	1	2	3	4

Individuals are close and share many levels of their personality.

0	1	2	3	4

Social distance reduced.

0	1	2	3	4

Moderately close if bounds of propriety are strictly maintained.

0	1	2	3	4

Great distance based on Not OK feelings of helplessness.

0	1	2	3	4

14. ACCURACY OF PERCEPTIONS OF SUPERIORS AND SUBORDINATES OF EACH OTHER

Inaccurate based on political considerations and desire to look strong.	Realistic and accurate based on open exchange of data and new learnings.	Little reality testing. Mostly "gut" reaction.	Accurate with tendency to pigeon-hole people and not test perceptions.	Inaccurate, based on projections, fantasy, wish, and "pleasing" behavior.
0 1 2 3 4	0 1 2 3 4	0 1 2 3 4	0 1 2 3 4	0 1 2 3 4

15. CONCERN OF SENIORS ABOUT PROBLEMS FACED BY JUNIORS

Could care less. Assumes he knows best.	Concern actively expressed in attempts to understand subordinates and their problems.	Interested in pleasure and rewards for self.	Concern based on principles of leadership rather than empathy.	All energy consumed with own Not OKness.
0 1 2 3 4	0 1 2 3 4	0 1 2 3 4	0 1 2 3 4	0 1 2 3 4

B.

B	P-S	S/C	BC	D

16. LEVEL IN COMPANY WHERE DECISIONS ARE MADE

Decisions are made as close to the problem as possible by those who have resources necessary for resolution.

0	1	2	3	4

Policies are formulated at the top with more specific decisions made at lower levels but checked with top before action.

0	1	2	3	4

Decisions are avoided as long as possible at all levels.

0	1	2	3	4

Decisions made at all levels but neither with use of others resources nor consideration of consequences for others.

0	1	2	3	4

Decisions are bucked upstairs and made at the top.

0	1	2	3	4

17. ACCURACY OF INFORMATION AVAILABLE TO DECISION-MAKERS

Accurate information is complete as possible based on careful collection processes and open flow of information.

0	1	2	3	4

Bad news is with-held while good news gets wide distribution.

0	1	2	3	4

Information is distorted, highly filtered, and chaotic.

0	1	2	3	4

Information is intuitive and disorganized.

0	1	2	3	4

Information is highly colored, prejudiced, and of doubtful validity.

0	1	2	3	4

18. EXTENT DECISION-MAKERS INVOLVE OTHERS IN THE DECISION-MAKING PROCESS

Senior person goes it alone because he knows best.
0 | 1 | 2 | 3 | 4

Creative and energetic people are asked to give input.
0 | 1 | 2 | 3 | 4

Only those are approched who already agree.
0 | 1 | 2 | 3 | 4

A few trusted aides are involved in decision-making.
0 | 1 | 2 | 3 | 4

All who can contribute to the solution are given access to the problem.
0 | 1 | 2 | 3 | 4

19. EXTENT PROFESSIONAL COMPETENCE SOUGHT IN DECISION-MAKING

Third parties scorned.
0 | 1 | 2 | 3 | 4

Ideas and those who create them cause organizational excitement.
0 | 1 | 2 | 3 | 4

Because of helplessness or rebelliousness, sees no worth in others' resources.
0 | 1 | 2 | 3 | 4

Others' comptence questioned.
0 | 1 | 2 | 3 | 4

Third party professional and technical competence used to bring new insights into organization.
0 | 1 | 2 | 3 | 4

20. EXTENT DECISION-MAKERS AWARE OF PROBLEMS IN OTHER PARTS OF THE ORGANIZATION

Well acquainted with problems at all levels.	Aware but uninvolved with certitude they could do it better.	Uses others' problems as a way to avoid dealing with own.	Concern for problems of others without action.	Scornful of problems of others.
0 1 2 3 4	0 1 2 3 4	0 1 2 3 4	0 1 2 3 4	0 1 2 3 4

21. USE OF MEMBER RESOURCES IN DECISION-MAKING

Concensus is sought among all those related to the problem.	It is expected top-side gets paid for making decisions.	People and decisions are avoided and ignored.	Resources are used when creative energy is flowing.	Decisions are made only at the top.
0 1 2 3 4	0 1 2 3 4	0 1 2 3 4	0 1 2 3 4	0 1 2 3 4

22. EXTENT SUBORDINATES INFLUENCE DECISIONS RELATED TO THEIR WORK

Subordinates involved where appropriate, and all information available to them.	Subordinates are consulted but not involved in the decision itself.	Subordinates are only aware of their immediate needs and don't see larger problems.	Creative subordinates can influence work issues. Not regularly consulted.	Decisions are handed down without comment.
0 1 2 3 4	0 1 2 3 4	0 1 2 3 4	0 1 2 3 4	0 1 2 3 4
P-S	BC	D	S/C	B

C.

23. LEVELS IN THE ORGANIZATION WHERE CONTROL OPERATES MOST EFFECTIVELY

Largely at the top with some feeling of responsibility at lower levels.	All levels function autonomously with easy interfacing.	Control tends to gravitate upwards.	Control tends to move downward and be shared throughout the organization.	Organization largely out of control. Rumors and scapegoating are prevalant at all levels.
0 1 2 3 4	0 1 2 3 4	0 1 2 3 4	0 1 2 3 4	0 1 2 3 4

24. ACCURACY OF MEASUREMENTS AND CONTROL DATA

Strong need to insulate self and colleagues from bad news.

0	1	2	3	4

Tendency to use experimentation and "gut" reactions rather than data.

0	1	2	3	4

Strong defensive forces at work to distort information in order to protect image of success.

0	1	2	3	4

Measurement data, and well-organized factual reports, shared throughout organization.

0	1	2	3	4

Strong pressures at work to distort and falsify information to immunize individuals from reality.

0	1	2	3	4

25. USE OF CONTROL INFORMATION

Used to reward productivity and for guidance in response to issued orders.

0	1	2	3	4

Control information treated with an OK attitude and viewed with humor.

0	1	2	3	4

Largely used to coerce, police and punish.

0	1	2	3	4

Used for self-control and for team guidance in problem-solving.

0	1	2	3	4

Either ignored or used to punish, "get even" and play "Gottcha".

0	1	2	3	4

26. INFLUENCE OF INFORMAL NETWORK

	0	1	2	3	4
May support or subtly resist organizational goals.	0	1	2	3	4
May appear resistant because outspoken. Supports organizational goals.	0	1	2	3	4
Cynical about and resistant to organizational goals.	0	1	2	3	4
All energy directed toward achievement of organizational goals.	0	1	2	3	4
Concerned only about its own goals and security.	0	1	2	3	4

27. CONCENTRATION OF PERFORMANCE APPRAISAL FUNCTIONS

	0	1	2	3	4
Used by top management to show good will and avoided when news is bad.	0	1	2	3	4
Used throughout organization whenever appropriate as a creative tool for positive and negative feedback.	0	1	2	3	4
Concentrated in top management and used to punish.	0	1	2	3	4
Takes place at all levels of organization including lower level appraisal of senior management.	0	1	2	3	4
Concentrated in top management. Used to reward cronies or punish "outgroup".	0	1	2	3	4

BC   S/C   B   P-S   D

28. EXPRESSION BY SUPERIORS OF TRUST AND CONFIDENCE IN SUBORDINATES

Openness and willingness to take risks with people and share responsibility.

0	1	2	3	4

Tend to act as if subordinates don't exist.

0	1	2	3	4

Trust accompanied with reluctance to surrender control functions. Subordinates treated paternalistically.

0	1	2	3	4

Tend to see subordinates as incompetent and in need of direction.

0	1	2	3	4

Tend to be trusting of creative subordinates who generate energy in others. Likes and dislikes are immediately visible.

0	1	2	3	4

29. SUBORDINATES' TRUST AND CONFIDENCE IN SUPERIORS

Realistic understanding of the limitations of power and the interdependence of all people.

0	1	2	3	4

Servile to boss until experiencing defeat, then rebellious. Game: "See What You Made Me Do".

0	1	2	3	4

Incomplete. Keeps working at it as a business ideal.

0	1	2	3	4

Faultfinding is big. Game: "If It Weren't For Them I Could".

0	1	2	3	4

Lets superiors immediately know when agree or disagree.

0	1	2	3	4

30. EXPRESSION OF CARING

Appropriately intimate in all situations. Caring is legitimated throughout the organization.

0	1	2	3	4

Attitude: "Nobody cares about me, so why should I be concerned about others?"

0	1	2	3	4

Giving strokes and nurturing usually around business issues and in the service of friendship.

0	1	2	3	4

Support behavior is patronizing and ritualistic. Puts people down.

0	1	2	3	4

Gives spontaneous, positive strokes and readily accepts them, but not always appropriate to work situation.

0	1	2	3	4

31. FREEDOM OF SUBORDINATES TO APPROACH SUPERIORS TO DISCUSS WORK ISSUES

Discuss work related issues with superiors in problem-solving atmosphere.

0	1	2	3	4

So concerned with own "act" has no energy for problems.

0	1	2	3	4

Talk upwards is restrained. Expect to be patronized but not receive useful help.

0	1	2	3	4

Asking for help is seen as weak and invites put-downs.

0	1	2	3	4

May impulsively use ingenious approaches.

0	1	2	3	4

32. USE OF SUBORDINATES' IDEAS IN PROBLEM-SOLVING

Seniors openly solicit and use ideas, opinions, and feelings of juniors.

0	1	2	3	4

Subordinates' ideas are viewed as useless.

0	1	2	3	4

Seniors friendly with juniors but expect no meaningful ideas.

0	1	2	3	4

Seniors expect subordinates to do what they are told.

0	1	2	3	4

Seniors seek ideas of some creative juniors with whom they enjoy developing options.

0	1	2	3	4

33. FREEDOM OF SUPERIORS TO ASK HELP FROM SUBORDINATES

Superiors openly seek help and take into account opinions, ideas and feelings of subordinates.

0	1	2	3	4

They're too busy anticipating problems. Games: "Ain't I Wonderful" or "Look How Hard I'm Trying."

0	1	2	3	4

Superiors hide their "flatsides" and operate from the "rescuer" position.

0	1	2	3	4

Superiors assume they are smarter than subordinates.

0	1	2	3	4

Superiors spontaneously seek help.

0	1	2	3	4

34. FREEDOM OF SUBORDINATES TO ASK FOR HELP ON WORK ISSUES FROM SUPERIORS

It is realistically assumed everyone is committed to his own growth.	To please their superiors. They expect to be ignored.	The norm is everyone must stand on his own feet.	Fear of exposing themselves by revealing weaknesses. Fear of being put down.	Asking may be inappropriate.
0 1 2 3 4	0 1 2 3 4	0 1 2 3 4	0 1 2 3 4	0 1 2 3 4

35. FREEDOM OF PEERS TO ASK EACH OTHER FOR HELP

They value "differencing" and understand the value of collaboration.	Cynically done as an invitation to a game of "See What You Made Me Do" or in a way to get a "no" response.	Need to appear superior by working independently.	Afraid others might get credit for their work.	Help offered in a playful, half serious way.
0 1 2 3 4	0 1 2 3 4	0 1 2 3 4	0 1 2 3 4	0 1 2 3 4

E.

P-S   D   BC   B   S/C

36. CHARACTERISTIC TRANSACTION

Punishing Parent to Child

0	1	2	3	4

Nurturing Parent to Child

0	1	2	3	4

Adult to Adult

0	1	2	3	4

Child to Child

0	1	2	3	4

Adapted Child to Parent

0	1	2	3	4

37. CHARACTER OF PREDOMINANT TRANSACTIONS

Judgemental, loud, and critical in nature.

0	1	2	3	4

Condescension by superiors and caution by subordinates.

0	1	2	3	4

Friendly, fostering openness, trust and confidence. Direct.

0	1	2	3	4

Playful, creative, spontaneous, and noisy. Energetic.

0	1	2	3	4

Defensive with whining or blaming.

0	1	2	3	4

38. PRESENCE OF TEAMWORK

Viewed as ineffective and time wasting.
| 0 | 1 | 2 | 3 | 4 |

Among peers "rescuing" rather then open exchange.
| 0 | 1 | 2 | 3 | 4 |

Present at all levels of the organization.
| 0 | 1 | 2 | 3 | 4 |

Extensive network of informal cooperation related or unrelated to company goals.
| 0 | 1 | 2 | 3 | 4 |

Unresolved agenda churning around impedes working together.
| 0 | 1 | 2 | 3 | 4 |

39. EXTENT TO WHICH SUBORDINATES CAN INFLUENCE ORGANIZATIONAL GOALS AND METHODS

Communication flow restricted. Subordinates are expected to stay in their place.
| 0 | 1 | 2 | 3 | 4 |

Subordinates are expected to work and managers to plan.
| 0 | 1 | 2 | 3 | 4 |

Participant goal-setting used throughout organization.
| 0 | 1 | 2 | 3 | 4 |

Goals are unclear and changing. Job descriptions vague.
| 0 | 1 | 2 | 3 | 4 |

The lower you are the less valuable you feel.
| 0 | 1 | 2 | 3 | 4 |

40. AMOUNTS OF CONTROL MANAGERS HAVE OVER ACTIVITIES OF THEIR DEPARTMENTS

Thought to be substantial but actually only moderate. Resistance expressed in games and politics.	Moderate to substantial based on benevolent control strategies.	Substantial when rank and status are complemented with knowledge and competence.	Moderate to substantial. A lot is "happening" and it may not be control.	Unit looks more like a gang than an organization.
0 1 2 3 4	0 1 2 3 4	0 1 2 3 4	0 1 2 3 4	0 1 2 3 4

41. COOPERATION BETWEEN DEPARTMENTS

Others exist to be blamed and used in politics and games.	Between horizontal groups; less in vertical relationships.	Other departments or 3rd parties seen as resources to decision-making.	Depends on the subject and mood.	Value of organization is discounted.
0 1 2 3 4	0 1 2 3 4	0 1 2 3 4	0 1 2 3 4	0 1 2 3 4

F.   B   BC   P-S   S/C   D

42. UNDERLYING MOTIVATIONAL NEEDS

Need to win and need for structure. Desire to be liked and/or different.

0	1	2	3	4

Need for affiliation, achievement, creative expression, recognition, autonomy, and pleasure.

0	1	2	3	4

Use of full range of ego state motivations plus motivational forces found in cohesive groups.

0	1	2	3	4

Need for economic security, status, achievement, and affiliation.

0	1	2	3	4

Need for structure and security, especially financial. Desire for status and power.

0	1	2	3	4

43. MANNER IN WHICH INCENTIVES ARE USED

In-group members receive rewards while out-group members are continually put-down.

0	1	2	3	4

Hugs and bugs shared freely around.

0	1	2	3	4

Economic and all three ego state motivations are used in joint goal setting and process management.

0	1	2	3	4

Acceptance given to those who go along and withheld from those who differ.

0	1	2	3	4

Fear, threats of punishment and occasional rewards.

0	1	2	3	4

44. MEMBER ATTITUDE TOWARD ORGANIZATION

	0	1	2	3	4
Indifference or passive resistance to organization's goals.					
Enthusiastic and favorable when things go well.					
Positive and upbeat. Strongly motivated to achieve organization's goals.					
Both hostile and favorable with consonant motivation to achieving organization's goals.					
Angry, hurt, and defensive with energy going into blaming rather than organization's goals.					

45. EXTENT TO WHICH CONFLICT IS SURFACED

	0	1	2	3	4
Denied, repressed, and active beneath the surface.					
Tends to surface explosively. May be creatively dealt with.					
Accepted, surfaced, identified, and resolved.					
Tends to be smoothed over and overlooked rather than resolving the underlying issues.					
Seen as inevitable and agreement impossible; even encouraged so can look strong.					

46. INDIVIDUAL "OWNERSHIP" OF ORGANIZATIONAL GOALS

	0	1	2	3	4
Individuals are too busy doing whatever they're told or fighting the system to feel responsible.	0	1	2	3	4
"This place really turns me on."	0	1	2	3	4
Individuals at all levels feel responsible for organizational goals and actively support them.	0	1	2	3	4
Managerial personnel feel responsible. Game: "I'm Only Trying To Help". Rank and file feel no responsibility.	0	1	2	3	4
Senior levels feel responsible, but accuse lower levels of not being committed; middle levels less so. Lower levels may restrain production.	0	1	2	3	4

47. ATTITUDES OF INDIVIDUALS TOWARD OTHER ORGANIZATION MEMBERS

	0	1	2	3	4
Subservient and expectation meeting.	0	1	2	3	4
Openly and directly express likes and dislikes to superiors, peers and subordinates.	0	1	2	3	4
Supportive and collaborative attitudes throughout organization fostering trust and mutual confidence.	0	1	2	3	4
Cooperative and favorable attitudes toward others; competition among peers plus distrust and condescension toward subordinates.	0	1	2	3	4
Servility toward superiors mixed with fear; hostility toward peers and contempt for subordinates. Trust is conspicuously absent.	0	1	2	3	4

48. SATISFACTION DERIVED FROM WORK

	Dissatisfaction arising from corrosive competition, destructive behavior and stroke starvation.	"My work is a source of joy."	Satisfaction at all levels based on trust, participation, achievement and recognition.	Satisfaction with regard to membership, recognition, supervision, and little with regard to work itself.	Dissatisfaction and absence of a sense of achievement and recognition related to work.
	0 1 2 3 4	0 1 2 3 4	0 1 2 3 4	0 1 2 3 4	0 1 2 3 4

G.

D	S/C	P-S	BC	B

49. INDIVIDUAL MEMBER COMMITMENT TO OWN PROFESSIONAL GROWTH

Aculturating oneself to the organization.	Commitment to serve the organization better.	Overwhelmed by sense of defeat and hopelessness.	Commitment to what is pleasurable and creative.	Committed to their professional and interpersonal skill development.
0 1 2 3 4	0 1 2 3 4	0 1 2 3 4	0 1 2 3 4	0 1 2 3 4

50. MANAGEMENT'S ENCOURAGEMENT OF PROFESSIONAL TRAINING

Bonus for outstanding achievers. May be seen as potential threat.	Considered for everyone but only those few encouraged who have a "future" with the company.	Valuable only to further the narrowest company goals.	Encouragement for latest fad may soon turn into disinterest.	Assumption is organization can't grow if people don't grow.
0 1 2 3 4	0 1 2 3 4	0 1 2 3 4	0 1 2 3 4	0 1 2 3 4

51. ADEQUACY OF TRAINING RESOURCES PROVIDED

Poor and educational strategies out-moded.	Adequate to maintain present level or organizational competence but no room for experimentation.	Poor and seen as a waste of time and money.	Adequate but tend to be used sporadically.	Excellent and research and experimentation are encouraged.
0 1 2 3 4	0 1 2 3 4	0 1 2 3 4	0 1 2 3 4	0 1 2 3 4

H.

B	BC	D	S/C	P-S

52. EXTENT TO WHICH JOB DESCRIPTIONS ARE CLEARLY DEFINED

Some people do whatever's at hand in order to please.

0 1 2 3 4

Duties and responsibilities shift depending on what the hot issue is.

0 1 2 3 4

Individual's job responsibilities and goals seem to mesh with everyone elses. Unit goals seen as most important.

0 1 2 3 4

Job descriptions and achievement goals are handed down based on past history.

0 1 2 3 4

Job responsibility and achievement goals jointly arrived at and regularly monitored.

0 1 2 3 4

53. IMMEDIACY OF FEEDBACK ON PERFORMANCE

Inconsistant, and irregular and irrelevant to the employee.

0 1 2 3 4

Sporatic in timing and lacking in consistency.

0 1 2 3 4

Given indirectly and without regards to employee learning.

0 1 2 3 4

Erratic, negating, and blaming.

0 1 2 3 4

Systems are established that give immediate and consistant feedback to employee on how well he is doing.

0 1 2 3 4

54. PERFORMANCE APPRAISAL AS A LEARNING EXPERIENCE

Employee feels powerless and abused.

| 0 | 1 | 2 | 3 | 4 |

A creative exchange.

| 0 | 1 | 2 | 3 | 4 |

"Nice guy" approach. "One big happy family" approach. Irrelevant to learning.

| 0 | 1 | 2 | 3 | 4 |

Employee feels defensive, embarrassed, and "on the carpet".

| 0 | 1 | 2 | 3 | 4 |

Timely and mutual discussion of the issues and problems of work and the organization.

| 0 | 1 | 2 | 3 | 4 |

55. LEVEL AT WHICH SUPERVISORS SET GOALS FOR ORGANIZATION TO ACHIEVE

Discussion of goals is avoided altogether.

| 0 | 1 | 2 | 3 | 4 |

Goals are a sometime thing which may be very provocative.

| 0 | 1 | 2 | 3 | 4 |

High with benevolent approach.

| 0 | 1 | 2 | 3 | 4 |

High and unrealistic so boss will appear powerful.

| 0 | 1 | 2 | 3 | 4 |

Goals are set to challenge employee's best efforts, and within context of organization's mission and resources.

| 0 | 1 | 2 | 3 | 4 |

I.

D   S/C   BC   B   P-S

SCORING THE ORGANIZATIONAL PROFILE

1. Add (downward) the scores for each cell within each of the nine alphabetically designated categories. Place the sums provided in the boxes at the end of each division. (ie. designated A through I)

2. Transfer the sub-division totals to the score sheet below. Be sure to match the five cell designations B with B, S/C with S/C and so forth.

3. Add the nine cells on the score sheet and place the totals in the boxes marked "cell totals".

4. Add together only the figures in the two right hand cells (marked by circles) and place this total in the square marked "profile score".

5. To create a visual profile, draw a line across the column marked "Blaming" at the point that corresponds to the actual score. Do the same for columns marked "Benign Control", "Problem-solving", "Spontaneous/Creative" and "Distracting". Crosshatch all columns below your marks.

SCORING SHEET

A.

B   BC   P-S   S/C   D

B.

B   BC   P-S   S/C   D

C.

B   BC   P-S   S/C   D

D.

B   BC   P-S   S/C   D

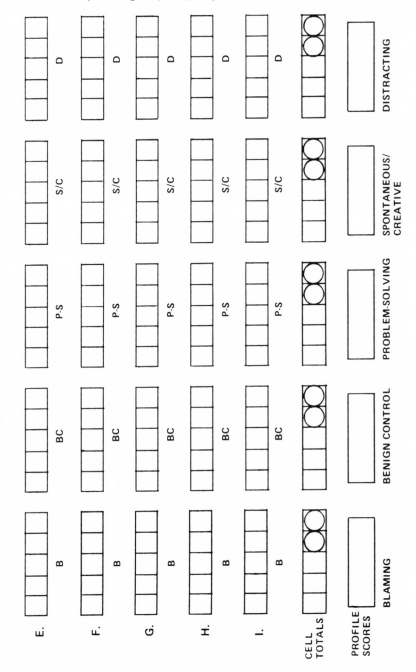

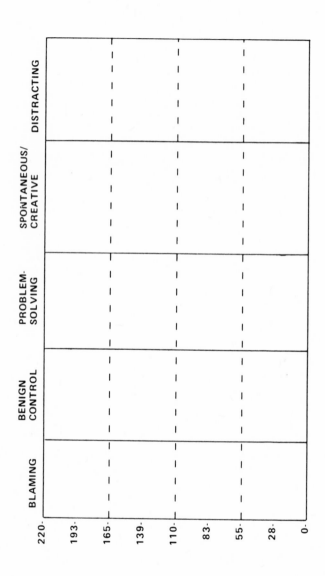

PROFILE SCORE

BLAMING BENIGN CONTROL PROBLEM-SOLVING SPONTANEOUS/CREATIVE DISTRACTING

220 193 165 139 110 83 55 28 0

INTERPRETATION OF RESULTS

Experience demonstrates there is an internal scale in the five organizational systems. It is the relative amount of rational energy that goes into problem solving and the here-and-now quality of deliberations. On the one hand, the scale as it moves from Problem-solving through Benign Control toward Blaming devolves toward prejudice and rigidity. In this profile, increasing amounts of energy are spent in maintaining the status quo and in defending against change. On the other hand, as the scale moves from Problem-solving through Spontaneous/Creative to Distracting there is a devolution toward delusory and chaotic behavior. Research suggests there are four profiles from which a number of other profiles can be extrapolated.

CONVEX PROFILE

HIGH: Problem-Solving
MEDIUM: Benign Control and Spontaneous/Creative
LOW: Blaming and Distracting

This profile represents the most functional organization. It is able to muster the most rational horsepower on the problem. While attempting to maintain a flexible organization and open process, it does not lose sight of its real purpose and goals. Since organizations can't grow if people don't, it makes intelligent efforts to manage its human resource. It values "different" people and fresh approaches, which it integrates into the ongoing life of the company. Control (Problem-solving) tends to take place as close to the problem as possible. Punishment is progressive and remedial whenever possible.

Other aspects of the Convex Organization include:

Power of rank complemented by that of competence.
Authentic caring (stroking) present.

Ethical concerns consciously dealt with.

Resistance to convergent thinking.

Training activities are prominent.

Incentive compensation programs.

High trust and easy flow of information.

Wide use of third-party resources.

Creative fight style.

Recognition, achievement, and advancement are part of compensation program.

CONCAVE PROFILE

HIGH: Blaming and Distracting
MEDIUM: Benign Control and Spontaneous/Creative
LOW: Problem-solving

This profile represents an organization that is unnecessarily difficult to deal with. When production sales and labor relations go well, things proceed on a reasonably even keel. But when the indicators turn down, instead of powering-up intelligence, we see alarms, recriminations, tension, rumors, pressurized meetings, threats, and even firings. Firefighting is the name of the game. Because functional intelligence is low, even when things go well, there are undercurrents of apprehension as people anticipate the next explosion. The absence of planning, problem solving, and stroking ensures that there is another nemesis to be faced around a future bend in the road.

Other aspects of the Concave Organization include:

Punishment is retributive and demotivating.

Structure tends to be rigid.

Lower levels use informal networks to frustrate company designs.

Self-protection is necessary.

Legalistic approach substitutes for problem solving.
Communication is only downward and usually threatening.
Upward communication is distorted (figures fudged).
Production and quality are erratic.
"Key people" play increasingly important roles.
Employee "ownership" of company goals is low.

LEFT SLOPE PROFILE

HIGH: Blaming
MEDIUM: Benign Control and Problem-solving
LOW: Spontaneous/Creative and Distracting

This is the classic old-style, power-on, authority-obedient organization. All responsibility and power are seen to be on the top. When things go wrong, blame is shared around. It is presumed that there is a correlation between rank in organization and competence. There are often "in" and "out" groups and hazing takes place. Information flow may be so restricted that it becomes "management by secrecy." Planning may be present, but "how we've always done it" maintenance of the status quo is controlling. Organizational rank and hierarchical perquisites may be strictly defined and observed. Among senior managers there may be no correlation between their contribution and their salary. Subordinates tend to be compliant and to meet expectations.

Other aspects of a Left Slope Organization include:

Industrial engineering is important.
Focus is on immediate future (tomorrow).
Control is often punitive.
Politics and games are everywhere.
Atmosphere is indifferent to hostile.
Discounting is present.

RIGHT SLOPE PROFILE

HIGH: Spontaneous/Creative and Distracting
MEDIUM: Problem-solving and Benign Control
LOW: Blaming

This profile represents a high-energy organization sensitive to social or market changes. People are "on stage" a lot. Creativity is an organizational buzzword. Noise levels may be high and behavior flamboyant, with a tendency for things to become chaotic. Often an indifference to traditional codes of dress and behavior appears. Moments or products of great success may become benchmarks. Often unit loyalty is low and leadership rotates in and out of the company.

Other aspects of a Right Slope Organization include:

There are rewards for bright people and their efforts.
A lunatic fringe may develop.
Focus is strongly on today, not yesterday or tomorrow.
Atmosphere may be "hyper."
It is often a fun place to be.
There is a concern for fresh faces and ideas.
Wide tolerance of individual differences is encouraged.
Feelings are commonly expressed.

4

The Development Model

An organization functions at four levels simultaneously. They are (1) the problems it attempts to face and resolve; (2) the style used as members go about it; (3) the contribution of individual member behavior; and (4) motivations below members' level of awareness. We refer to these levels as:

1. Problem solving.
2. Process management.
3. Behavior training.
4. Motivational activities.

In a development program, most organizational energy goes into problem solving. Process matters are dealt with only if and when they impede problem solving. When behavior drags down process, it is brought into consideration. Motivational matters are considered when they influence behavior negatively. The lower levels of the model are dealt with to improve the functioning of the higher levels.

The model also represents one way the total development effort proceeds over time. Workers and managers find it easiest to talk about business matters. Process matters, when they arise, usually evoke energetic and easy participation. Discussion of behavior and its consequences comes harder and occurs only when members have a growing sense of trust and confidence. Motivational assumptions and activities are ordinarily the last to be encountered.

One basic use of the model is to help workers see that problems occur at different levels. If you don't understand the problem at the level it occurs or attempt to solve it at the wrong level, your efforts will misfire. In order to be successful, all parties have to talk on the same level. If company norms support only secrecy and games, it isn't helpful to encourage a worker to be more direct and open. The consequences would be counterproductive. In this instance, the worker isn't the problem. The style of the work group is. Asking workers to change without changing the system will be a failure and will separate them from their peers.

LEVEL 1: PROBLEM SOLVING

Problem solving is the means of exposing team process and member behavior, plus the measure of the quality and quantity of work done. The problems dealt with are those indigenous to the organization at the point the development program begins. The problems run the gamut of business experience. When the development effort is fully on track, each level of the organization is meeting and solving those problems before it.

The goal is collaboration with high energy and consciousness, high data flow, and transactions marked by open and vigorous give-and-take. This takes time to achieve in the face of a general cynicism about the value of social life. A formal problem-solving technique may be introduced, like critical pathing or a planning and decision model. The real energy is placed on the implications of group process, member behavior, and motivational dynamics operating below members' level of awareness. These are levels 2, 3, and 4.

LEVEL 2: PROCESS MANAGEMENT

All companies and their subunits have a recognizable culture, style, or process—that is, a characteristic way of confronting a variety of activities. This culture takes concrete expression in work rules, organizational structuring, strategies, values, rites of entrance and exit, and ways of making decisions. A company style includes shared attitudes toward a variety of subjects such as unions, technology, sex roles, and the importance of R&D.

Culture is the primary determinant of people's behavior. Behavior is the consequence of the culture in which it occurs and not of such unvalidated constructs as personality, character, will power, instinct, and sinfulness. Conditions in the environment collectively determine behavior, not states of mind inside us. This points to one of the sources of the regularity of human behavior. It occurs not because of the responses fashioned in the here and now, but rather because of consequences that have followed from similar behavior in the past. Behavior remains constant because culture does. Behavior fits the environment. The goal of process management is to make the social structure that informs behavior available to management, in the same way any business problem is.

Psychologists attempt to discover the behavior of mice and other small animals by putting them in a maze in search of food. In a series of trials, they observe the rodents' learning thresholds, levels of frustration, relearning capacities, and the like. They are studying mice. We are interested not so much in mice as in the structure of the maze in which they operate. Situations powerfully influence people's opinions, feelings, and behavior. They may not be aware of this and may feel powerless to influence the "maze." Our task is to discover the makeup of the maze and its influence on employee behavior. By making culture available to managers and workers, we create "maze-bright" employees.

Process, which is the operational form of culture, directly influences the adequacy of decision making. Good process equals good problem solving. Poor process drains off vital energy into games and politics—energy which then is not available for problem solving. Some units are despoiled by bad process. They must spend so much energy coping with bad process that they are unable to meet the challenges of the marketplace. They go the way of W. T. Grant.

Organizations proceed through three fairly defined steps as they bring their process under control. They are (1) discovery, (2) discharge, and (3) definition.

Discovery is the "aha" experience of finding the maze—of discovering organizational style. Often the discovery is accompanied with a surprised "You mean we can talk about it?" Gales of laughter rock the room as members own up to their own versions of "If the president doesn't see it, it doesn't exist," or "If I say a thing three times it's true," or "What—I made a mistake? I haven't made one mistake in six years," or "I don't know why you think I'm angry just because my face is purple." These were games and stratagems workers devised to deal with the secrecy, fear, and control that characterized old-style companies. It was necessary to overlook much ridiculousness just to keep the old style going.

When organizational style is first discovered, it often has an unbelievable quality. As long as everyone goes along with the conspiracy not to see the obvious, behavior can become increasingly weird. Like the marketing vice-president who sought control by inviting subordinates to lunch at a local country club and publicly berating them. Or the sales head who could discipline subordinates only very late at night when he was thoroughly drunk.

As workers go through the process of discovering their past culture, a lot of discharging, correcting erroneous impressions, and reestablishing broken relationships takes place. This liberates energy for work. Discharging consists of reporting old angers, frustrations, and hurts that are still hanging around. It is a natural process. It should be faced with equanimity and allowed, indeed encouraged, to run its course. Everyone should be given an opportunity to tell his or her whole story and to get off it. When angers, confusions, and hurts are experienced fully, they disappear. The old Army saw that "a griping soldier is a happy soldier" was based on the insight that if people express their feelings they get free of them. Pent-up feelings have the same disruptive energy today that they had when they first occurred years ago. Workers should be encouraged to "let it all hang out"—once. The rule is: Everyone gets one absolutely free bitch. After that he or she must face and resolve the problem.

In the past, without an opportunity to discharge old hurts, workers had to construct strange fantasies and add interpretations in order to make some sense out of life and its frustrations. These distortions can be cleared up when people are allowed to report what happened to them. With a view of reality no longer blurred by past emotional sludge, people are free to see things as they are and take their place on the team. This leads directly to the reestablishing of broken relationships and communication links.

The third step in process management is definition. Team members begin to define what they desire the organization to be for them. There are no ideal types. Doubtless the definitions will include a lot of what has worked for them plus some new ideas they haven't tried before. The process involves workers and management joining together to deal with the reality of their work life and what they want from it. Individual contributions have to be heard, discussed, and tried. The time is one of trial and error. Members begin by accepting greater management over their joint responsibilities. They then set their personal growth goals and contract with each other for the new team results they desire. Members find themselves being stretched, and when they discover that the process is real, they enjoy it.

The following questions can help members define their own culture and contract for what they want in the future. The ten categories of questions cover what I believe to be the most significant variables.

1. *Goal setting.* How are goals set in the organization? What consequences does this have for motivation? Are goals realistic? Are unrealistic goals rejected? How effective are planning activities?

2. *Communications flow.* How much rational horsepower is brought to bear on problems? In what direction does communication flow? Is it open, free, and undistorted, or is it confined, restricted, and full of games? What is the social distance between superiors and subordinates? How much upward influence is there?

3. *Process management.* Are people really talking where they live? Are members accepting responsibility for the productivity of the group? Are process comments forthcoming?

4. *Decision making.* What is the decision-making process? How are member and external resources used? How accurate is the information available? Are decisions made close to the problems?

5. *Control.* How is power used in teams? How do workers and managers relate to each other? Are control data accurate and shared widely? What is the role of the informal network?

6. *Characteristic behavior.* What is the trust level in the organization? What is a characteristic transaction? What is the stroke economy? Has caring been legitimated? Are members able to spot and interrupt games? Are they able to ask for and give helpful help?

7. *Typical transactions.* What are the typical transactions? How many of the following occur between participants: Parent

to Parent, Parent to Child, Child to Child, Adult to Adult, and Child to Parent?

8. *Motivational forces.* What is the nature of motivational forces? Are incentives present, plus recognition and advancement for achievement? Is worker enrichment practiced? Are organizational goals widely owned in the company? Is productivity rewarded with greater responsibility?

9. *Training and development.* Are members committed to their own growth? Is management committed to development and training activities? What level of resources are supplied to this activity?

10. *Appraisal and coaching.* Are feedback and coaching continuous and positive? Is performance appraisal related to work planning, and is it a learning experience for both parties? How are performance, appraisal, and competition related?

When company culture is changed from old style to new style, the attention of the total organization must be captured quickly. This is best done by informing the entire workforce patiently and precisely just how the new process will include them. At this juncture it is not necessary that workers understand the assumptions, values, and benefits of new-style strategies. That will come later. Below are examples of three outstanding companies whose culture is clearly defined, with decisive positive consequences for employees.

Alpha Company is in the entertainment field and runs a number of entertainment parks. Graduates of Alpha University are carefully selected and patiently trained so they are always "on stage" with the public. Their committed, upbeat attitude is designed to ensure that whenever a family from any part of America arrives at the park, they will enjoy the same high-quality entertainment as other families. Alpha Company has been able to achieve an enviable record of high commitment and willingness to support the organization's goals. Basic elements of Alpha's training and support include the following:

1. Careful selection eliminates people unable or unwilling to meet standards.
2. Structure and techniques of training emphasize keeping work sites clean, bright, and appealing. There is an aura of success everywhere.
3. There is a marked reduction of social distance between management and workers. A flattened organization chart is characteristic of new style. All Alpha managers spend time each year in ordinary park jobs.
4. The organization's central mission is constantly held before members.
5. Supervision at all levels gives subordinates daily strokes.
6. Work teams, including supervisors, practice job rotation on a regular basis within the shift.
7. Name tags are worn so that workers can be addressed by their first names.
8. There is a dress code.
9. Work alone discriminates individuals by their contribution.

Alpha training is absolute in spirit. The focus is on the cost and benefits of membership in a totally competent organization designed to meet high goals on a daily basis. "Being on" is defined precisely and new employees are led through their expected behavior step by step. Moreover, each worker is thoroughly trained in all elements of his or her job. This includes how machinery operates, responsibilities of supervision, crowd control, and what to do in unusual circumstances. Pride in self, pride in membership in the Alpha organization, and pride in work are the payoff.

Beta Company, a consumer products manufacturer, is another astonishing example of the productivity of new-style culture. The founder began in 1918 with $50 in capital to make electric adapter plugs. Today the business has grown to 118 factories and 55 overseas companies, doing in excess of $7 billion in sales each year. The theme that permeates employee thinking is that the mission of Beta Company is not primarily profit, but the service of mankind. The goal is to make a contribution to the world in return for using its resources.

To meet its goals, the company seeks the greatest possible contribution from each employee. Emphasis is placed on the personal and professional growth of workers and executives alike. The objective is to create an environment in which an individual's job becomes his or her primary source of growth and self-esteem. The result is 83,000 dedicated employees who have set worldwide standards of cost-effectiveness. It is easy to be cynical about such a management philosophy and to see it as merely self-serving. However, the reality of growth, productivity, and quality remains—all from a highly integrated and motivated workforce responding to a carefully constructed culture.

The six objectives of Beta Company, stated below, are not wallpapering. They inform the company environment at all levels of policy and production. The return to society for the use of its resources takes three forms. First, the company manufactures highest-quality products at the lowest possible prices. Beta company's name worldwide has become synonymous with quality. Second, taxes paid to governments and dividends to shareholders distribute benefits to many thousands. Third, by continuing to spend money on technological development, the company seeks to ensure future contributions to society. These are traditional activities. It is the new-style perspective that has produced startling results.

1. *National service through industry.* Our purpose shall not be solely to gain wealth or to display industrial strength, but to contribute to the progress and welfare of the community and the nation.

2. *Fairness.* We shall be fair and just in all our business and

individual dealings. Without this spirit, we cannot win respect—nor can we respect ourselves, no matter how wise or capable we may be.

3. *Harmony and cooperation.* Alone we are weak; together we are strong. We shall work together as a family in mutual trust and responsibility. An association of talented people is but an unruly mob unless each member is imbued with the spirit of harmony.

4. *Struggle for betterment.* It shall be our policy to encourage trust and self-reliance so that each worker may gain self-respect through his or her own endeavor and struggle hard for betterment. Without this spirit, true peace and progress cannot be achieved.

5. *Courtesy and humility.* We shall respect the rights of others. We shall be cordial and modest. We shall praise and encourage freely. Without this spirit, there shall be no social order.

6. *Gratitude.* We shall repay the kindness of our associates, our community, our nation, and our foreign friends with gratitude. This spirit of gratitude will give us peace, joy, and unlimited strength to overcome all difficulties.

Gamma Company is familiar to all of us. It stands for what is definitive in Western technology. Gamma has a clearly defined culture derived from simpler days when employees sang songs to their managers and engineers from the company songbook. Because such behavior is viewed with suspicion today, a source of bonding between people has been lost. Gamma's culture influences worker and manager behavior every day. It molds people's sense of self and defines the parameters of their behavior.

Everyone associated with Gamma enjoys a feeling of success every day. Workers are pleased to report to others in the community that they work for Gamma. Pride can be heard in their apparent effort to diminish the importance of their association with Gamma. Their message is: "Lest you assume everyone who works for Gamma is superior, I want to make it clear I am just an ordinary person." Because of its success, Gamma can attract, pay, and hold the very best. It is easy to assume all Gamma managers are above average.

Company culture makes it clear that sales employees are due special respect. The company understands clearly that "nothing happens until someone sells something." In terms of recruiting, training, and remuneration, special attention is given to the sales force. Long-term employees are certain to highlight the time they have spent in sales. This is a credential of special merit.

There is a clearly defined dress code. I remember one day riding a Gamma Company elevator attired in my blue "sincere suit" and rep tie. I became aware of two men standing behind me who were discussing me. "He's been here so long he's beginning to look like us," one commented. "Yes," the other replied, "but he still wears brown wings." The occasion of much joking, the Gamma dress code helps create a positive self-image and influences people to participate fully.

Because of the high technology involved, Gamma is continually alert to new and emerging developments and makes this information available to employees. Indeed, the company would insist in the face of inertia that the new be tried. Gamma puts significant money behind its commitment to develop workers. Besides careful selection of new employees, it has a wage, salary, and benefit program that heads the market. Its determination to lead the field is felt in all decisions related to workers. Company buildings meet high standards of architectural design and landscaping excellence. Original works of art line many walls. A Gamma employee has strong motivation to work hard and prosper.

Gamma continually holds up to workers the importance of individual integrity and ethical awareness in all business transactions. Workers are encouraged to be active in civic affairs, where they can demonstrate to the community that Gamma employees, like the company itself, reflect the highest social concerns.

Obviously process or culture management is not new. I have said enough here, I believe, to establish how successful companies seek to structure their social environment to meet their corporate goals.

LEVEL 3: BEHAVIOR TRAINING

As a team works its process issues, members learn from each other and adjust their behavior to achieve those ends they seek for themselves. As a consequence, there is a general improvement in the overall functioning of the team. Generally each member's behavior is not noticeable unless the individual impairs problem solving. At this point behavior training is introduced to help members understand the piece of behavior confronting them. Another way of stating it is this: In order not to be controlled by the worst behavior in the room, workers are trained in behavior.

Behavior training is synonymous with Transactional Analysis. It is not the same as behavior modification. In behavior modification, people do not necessarily understand the dynamics of the behavior they are learning. In behavior training, all workers are trained at the same level in whatever they need to learn to manage their work. This is part of the no-mystery standard.

Behavior is what you see. It has to do with muscles, fascia, the circulatory system, and so forth. Eric Berne and other experimenters have made clear how our insides and outsides operate in synchronization. If you look carefully at people's outside when they transact with others, you will learn a lot about their inside.

Human behavior is highly regular in two ways. First, the dynamics of individual behavior are systematic and relatively constant. When a worker decides to build and maintain trust with co-workers, all activities in the category "things that build trust" will have their desired consequence. This is not a random finding. Speaking with candor tends to evoke candor. Compassion is irresistible. This refers, of course, to behavior that comes under the heading "normal." Pathological behavior, too, is constant; however, it proceeds by other dynamics.

Second, behavior is highly regular across the human species. What we know about behavior is not bound by culture or time. There may be wide differences of expression, but the basic dynamics remain the same worldwide. This is part of the radical social nature of human beings. People are tied inextricably to each other's destinies—and to the rest of the natural world. This is one of the insights that powers new-style organizations.

Behavior is best judged by its consequences. It is not good or bad in itself. Behavior is more a function of the organization in which it occurs than an outcome of individual insight, character, and will power. This idea may seem unusual, but it explains behavior more accurately than does the individualist approach. Even though group members see themselves as functioning individually, in reality they are responding to the assumptions, values, ideas, and goals of the organization.

In 1976, 300 cadets were expelled from West Point for violating the honor code. Of the explanations available for how such a large sample of America's finest young men failed to meet basic norms, only the above makes sense. Can you argue that somehow these 300 cadets were a bad sample? Do you suggest that there were a couple of sour apples that spoiled the barrel? Were the cultural and educational conditions such at that time to mislead these youngsters into shared bad journeys? Were their stars crossed? We strain for solutions that make no sense. The only credible answer is that something in the system itself caused the cadets to behave in a way for which they were punished.

We needn't look too hard to find the cause. The cadets were in a Catch-22 situation. Burdened with unrealistic work demands and time pressures, they arbitrarily increased their expectation levels. Stress mounted until they were forced to cope through extrasocietal behavior. No one experienced the total system, except possibly the cadets affected by it. The system was not realistically geared to their development needs. We can create systems that encourage openness and integrity, or we can mount those that guarantee members will lie, cheat, and steal. This holds in educational, political, or business organizations.

LEVEL 4: MOTIVATIONAL ACTIVITIES

Level 4 deals with motivation. It is the power behind behavior, below the worker's field of awareness. It contains the assumptions that undergird activities at all other levels. The generalization that workers are uncomfortable and unwilling to deal with theory does not prove out. On the contrary, workers appear fascinated by new-style assumptions and attracted to the dynamics of the unconscious. The progressive relaxation response (see Chapter 7) is one example. Most workers seem to enjoy exploring its implications for their personal and business lives. Since it deals with the most fundamental aspects of living, their interest is not surprising.

Given what most workers believe about themselves, social life, and others, it is not surprising that the majority are cynical about work. Implied in being a good administrator is maintaining the status quo. Survival is the best we can hope for. Because of these difficulties and the supposed scarcity of good management, coping well rather than growing is the hallmark of ability. Uncertainties, rapidly changing conditions, and myriad constraints lead managers to set reasonable rather than optimal targets. This mode of behavior has been described by Herbert Simon, 1978 Nobel laureate in economics, as "satisficing." What needs to happen for management and labor to play the game 100 percent? How can we equip members to give total effort? How can we reestablish the bonding of shared enterprise that makes it a joy to "take work to the limit"? How can we restore optimal standards of integration, communication, and productivity?

We first need to redefine what organizational life and group membership are all about. Older ideas have served us well. But in the postindustrial age some of these assumptions are no longer adequate to the task. As we experiment with new strategies, values, and tactics, we have to reexamine our traditional assumptions.

It is now clear from experience, research, and common sense that the question "How do we motivate workers?" is a deadend street. There isn't any way out of that corner. As long as we ask that question, or base our approach to work on it, we limit success. The real question is: "How do we remove those things that demotivate employees?" Basic to new-style management is the view that workers are already motivated. That's the way God created them. Our task is to create the conditions that allow them to be what they already are. This is a major shift in perspective. Below is a discussion of the assumptions that undergird new-style management.

NEW-STYLE ASSUMPTIONS ABOUT WORKERS

Cynicism about human endeavor runs deep in Western society. Taught to us at our parents' knee and reinforced periodically by violence and wars, we accept it as given. Some theologians have elevated the concept to the level of dogma, insisting on our "total depravity." This concept, whatever its source, fits nicely into the old-style way of viewing organizations. It sets the scene for those who proffer "man on a white horse" solutions to problems. If we start with cynicism about human endeavor and posit the essential corruption of human nature, we create a no-win situation. Failure is built into our efforts.

This is sufficient explanation for many of the critical organizational failures of our day. We are proceeding on assumptions that preset us for failure.

People are perfectly all right the way they are. The task is not to change them. People can conceive and execute plans sufficient to create stable, healthy, and happy working conditions. They can do whatever is necessary to create social systems that support the ecology of nature and that produce anxiety-free work environments and democratic political structures. Physicists have long demonstrated the elegance of the natural order. This elegance workers bring to work with them every morning.

The world works. God did not create a bummer. It is not a scam. We are not marks. People share in the elegance of nature. Our task is to put them in touch with what they already are. Over the centuries a number of thinkers have suggested that education does not consist of writing on a blank page. Education is not a teacher sticking information into the heads of pupils who later become teachers themselves. Rather, education is remembering what we always knew. It is recognition rather than discovery. It is a wise man (or woman), they say, who knows he doesn't need a teacher. Helping workers discover what they already know casts the training enterprise in a fresh light.

Workers are unaware of their own potential and have learned despair well. When told of their perfection, they are initially resistant and disbelieving and gradually become amazed and even angry. Only much later does the new reality become clear. When this happens, organizational change takes on the quality of transformation. New things begin to happen. The curse of Adam is lifted and the potential of joy is returned to work.

A manager creates space for employees by establishing the condition whereby they are able to expand control of larger segments of their work lives. The manager makes power available to them to solve problems and create the healthy work environment they desire. In doing so, the manager does not lose power. Paradoxically, when power is shared, there is more around for everyone. Power shrinks when it is held and grows when it is shared.

An officer of a large corporation called me to discuss a development program for first-line managers of a large petrochemical complex in Texas. He felt something was needed. Supervisory staff had largely surrendered management responsibility to the union. During recent grievance hearings it was sometimes unclear which side they were on. He was explicit on the following point:

> We don't want any theory. Our employees are practical types. Most of them never finished school. They don't know how to think. It would only upset them. We want to help them do their jobs better. We don't want to confuse them. What they need is a few techniques. They are practical people concerned only with the immediate. What they need is technique and practice.

Such a statement includes a number of negative assumptions about workers. The manager had really bagged himself. When you start out with such assumptions, you don't have far to go before you defeat yourself. If you are certain of the likelihood of failure before you begin, it's not hard to predict the probable outcome. Since this manager held cynical assumptions, he limited employees' potential for development.

The officer from the oil company misunderstood the usefulness of teaching theory. Several things were wrong with his position:

1. You can't build long-term relationships on technique alone. It is impossible to establish trust when people allow themselves only casual relationships. The rewards of loyalty and the bonding of "survivors" are not available to those who do not keep their agreements.
2. Soundly based insights are the soil in which future

growth takes place. Reality grasped today is a friend beside you, ready to be tested in the future.

3. No change worthy of the name takes place quickly. Everything worthwhile takes time. Nothing replaces persistence. Nothing is more common than unsuccessful people with talent.

4. Teaching workers techniques keeps them out of touch with their power. It is manipulative and feeds the idea of surrender and obedience rather than autonomy and responsibility.

Equally at variance with the commonplace is the new-style assumption that work systems offer people the potential to achieve their highest dignity. It is sobering to realize most workers simply have not had successful social experiences. Family, public schools, politics, the military, and business—all have received extensive media recognition, with examples of startling failures. That social systems are not seen as a value for responsible people to pursue was brought home to me recently on a flight to the coast. A fellow passenger reported, "I have spent my entire life arranging my work so as not to have to depend on other people. I have to do it alone." Other managers have admitted their frustration when they discovered that the higher they rose in the company the more their success was dependent on the efforts of others. These managers were unaware of the inverse proportion between rank in the organization and ability to succeed on one's own efforts.

"An ideal committee is composed of two people, one of whom is terminally ill." "If you want a job done right, do it yourself; if you don't care about the outcome, give it to a committee." There are few who see the profound error here. Most of us believe "If I'm lucky I'm born wealthy. Then I need other people only to command them." Because we have little successful social experience and do not hold corporateness as a value to be sought, we generate behavior that is excessively competitive, demotivating, and ultimately counterproductive. In denigrating social life we have sown the seeds of social chaos. Without clear assumptions about the value of social systems, we are exposed to those who espouse chaos via violence on both right and left. Workers simply are not experienced enough to see through this nihilism. They have no place to stand against the dictum that "out of chaos like the Phoenix the new order will arise." In business this know-nothingism is illustrated by cruel and destructive systems that feed off workers.

It is in social life that we achieve our highest dignity. If the choice has to be made between self and team, I opt for the team. Our lunar space shots were preeminent expressions of high technology and social integration. The Middle Ages, whatever its social abuses, was a period of high social integration, the value of whose artistic productions cannot be measured. Whatever people hope to achieve they can do so more effectively by working cooperatively. In the face of today's severe challenges we are going to have to discover deeper ways of collaborating to prevail. We need to rediscover what it means to be part of a whole and to function as a single unit.

It is a basic new-style assumption that we are social animals and at our deepest levels need to be connected to others. This "hooking" behavior reveals our highest urge and is the source of our greatest potency. Indeed, when we are isolated from society, for whatever reason, we tend to deteriorate emotionally, physically, and spiritually. Alienation and estrangement incapacitate us. Banishment and solitary confinement are the severest forms of noncapital political and communal punishment.

When we reflect on how human life is rooted in the biological, historical, geological, and astronomical fabric of nature, it is clear that all life is radically interdependent. We are not somehow more than the smallest of creatures. Nor are we less than the deepest reaches of space. We are simply part of it all. Countless intricate balances need to be maintained daily to allow us to continue our explorations and growth. Lewis Thomas in his delightful book points to some of the dazzling social realities.*

Synergism is the source of greatest potential for problem solving. As early as the second century Irenaeus of Lyon wrote of the synergism between God and humanity in creation. Synergism is the cooperative action taken by separate agencies so that the total effect is greater than the sum of the parts acting independently. When things synergize, two plus two equals much more than four. Procreation is synergy. Sperm and egg unite to produce a complex human being.

When a company synergizes, the result is a highly integrated organization where information flows freely with low distortion. A collective intelligence is formed that is far superior to the sum of individual knowledge. When a company synergizes, it has a superior power to adapt in the marketplace.

A development program is designed to enable workers to reach "critical mass," where synergism takes place. When that happens, people begin to grow. Individual excellence is a function of organizational excellence. As the majority of members exert their influence, an exciting thing happens. Transformation occurs. A new entity is formed. The transformation is experienced by workers at all levels and becomes a positive influence on customers. "Holistic" is a term used to describe this phenomenon. All parts of the system come together, they are connected and interconnected. Somehow things add up to more. Autonomy, authenticity, and passion are necessary ingredients. The synergistic organization is formidable. Its feats may be prodigious.

Another assumption that stands behind a development program concerns the meaning of leadership. New-style leadership uses control functionally to synchronize and fine-tune pro-

* Lewis Thomas, *The Lives of a Cell* (New York: Bantam Books, 1974).

cess, behavior, and motivation as well as the fundamentals of business. The analogy here is to a symphony and its conductor. Each musician has a different instrument and plays it according to his or her unique style. But under the guidance of the conductor, all synchronize their efforts to the whole.

Using the maximum resources available at any given moment, organizational leaders create a single work out of many parts. Synergism occurs when each worker responds to direction and synchronizes his or her effort to create an optimal group product. Power comes not from the leader, but from the members of the organization. Thus commitment to worker growth is fundamental. Workers provide the power that will enable companies to prevail in a time of rapid change.

What does this assume about workers? First, in an organization that is properly staffed each member is totally necessary. Functions and responsibilities will differ, but there are no second-class workers. Indeed, from time to time the company may be totally dependent on the least member. If he or she does not do the job right, the negative consequences may be far-reaching. It's the "for the want of a nail . . . the battle was lost" idea. Second, members need to see and listen to others. They need to be open to new ideas and committed to their own growth. It is counterproductive to frustrate their willingness to take increasing responsibility for larger pieces of the system. To limit employees is only to limit the organization. Third, space has to be created so members can play the game 100 percent. Workers have a much greater capacity for work than most management systems can handle.

Fourth, member differences of age, background, experience, talents, and training are valued. All contribute equally to the full, flavorful broth that is the organization. This is the source of the great inner beauty in powerful organizations and the source of the brilliant surprises we enjoy from time to time. The vision of continual growth is here. Finally, the indispensable quality of humor spices the mix. Humor is symptomatic of reality grounding. Workers who understand the ironies and paradoxes of life as well as the joy of winning and the pain of losing never can take themselves too seriously. They never quite get free of the stupendously humorous quality of things.

MOMENTS OF TRUTH

At different times and with varying impact, all who are involved in a development program experience a sense of awakening, discovery, or recognition. I describe this phenomenon as a moment of truth. Sometimes it strikes like a thunderclap and leaves the worker dazed and unable to assimilate its meaning. At times it is a gentle and confirming realization that steals upon the consciousness. At other times its arrival is a source of confusion, consternation, and chagrin. Challenging deeply held beliefs and fantasies, it may stimulate powerful internal conflicts. The worker becomes torn between the need to reject and the desire to accept new realities. Sometimes the new insight leaps full-blown into the mind, accompanied by a conviction the idea will work. If the new idea arrives in an easy way and if employees are given a chance to "live" with it, doubt it, and try it on for size, they may find a place for it in their lives. Another step has been taken forward.

Often there is a certain amount of pain in these discoveries. Workers need to realign their feelings and beliefs when they are upset by a new idea. They need time to digest the new concept, make behavior adjustments, and understand all the related facets. At such a juncture the leader must act so as not to overload workers. They need an opportunity to come to terms with the new learning. Each time people confront a new idea, they face the decision of rejecting it or exploring its possibilities. They may accept all, part, or none of it. If they are committed to their own learning, they welcome the confrontation, whatever they later decide to do with the new idea.

Below are some "moments of truth" workers need to come to grips with in a development program. These are functional changes an organization undergoes as it moves from old style to new, from closed to open, from distracting to nurturing, from unconscious to conscious.

When people see their own rigidity and undergo the discomfort associated with entertaining a new idea, they experience a moment of truth. The trainer may warn ahead of time what to expect and may also report humorous stories of others who initially lost the battle with a new idea. Nevertheless, when the new idea arrives, the person will experience discomfort and rejection. Taking responsibility to nurture oneself and to value play are two examples of such ideas. Early resisted, later they usually gain acceptance. People who have decided to face life with their own intelligence rather than with the archaic ideas of others will soon win this struggle. A moment of truth occurs when workers discover they can talk about the way they do things. There is a flash of insight as the "you mean we can talk about it" look spreads across their faces. This sometimes is followed by hilarity as members report their historical attempts to cope with the strangeness of many organizational norms. It's really a case of "the emperor has no clothes on."

One multinational company had no norms supporting collaboration. In the minds of managers collaboration was suspect, a sign of weakness; it was viewed as seditious by senior management. Regional managers began holding clandestine meetings to work together on common problems. To conceal their activities, they began to use pseudonyms and code words for meeting places. On the day they were able to bring their activities "in from the cold," the incongruity of the steps they had taken to solve company problems was met with hoots and hollers.

An important moment occurs in the development process when people discover the world works. Overlaid with games, rackets, and other coping strategies, barred by circumstances from authentic encounters, people understandably become cynical about work life. When cynicism sets in, they are left only with frustration as a coping mechanism and must seek such secondary benefits as may from time to time appear. Work then becomes a vast game controlled somewhere by someone, a kind of perpetual con in which all employees are marks.

When confronted with the power of strokes, the meaning behind words, and the opportunity to be open, tell the truth, and play the game 100 percent, workers at first experience surprise and excitement. This is quickly followed by anger and doubt. Anger will have to be discharged and trust built carefully over a period of time until the new idea is accepted. If this moment in development occurs, people regain zest and there is a release of energy into the system.

Such a moment of truth led to the failure of one development program at a Midwestern consumer goods plant. When supervisors reached the point where they could take responsibility for their work and tell the truth to each other, they became so excited they decided to hold an aftershift meeting to talk matters over. Fifty supervisors showed up on their own time. When company headquarters heard about the meeting, management went into shock. It could envision only bad things coming from such a meeting, such as a conspiracy or the formation of a union. Management ignored the whole thing and withdrew the program consultants. Those who attended the meeting got the message and the program was soon forgotten. Three years later there was a bitter six-week strike. Managers from headquarters traveled to the Midwest to discuss matters with the new plant manager. He reminded them that he had been a supervisor three years earlier when the development program was abandoned, and that he expected little help from them in the situation he faced. The premature rejection of the development program came back to haunt the organization.

A number of other discoveries await workers when they take responsibility for their lives and work. The discovery of their "act" is one. It is sobering to realize that we base our lives more on the archaic beliefs of others than on our own experience of reality. How our beliefs limit us and set us for failure is a startling recognition. So too is how we contribute to the pain of others. Rediscovering in the presence of others that cooperation, trust, and caring work can cause a disturbing excitement. Seeing process management for the first time and the consequences of interrupting games and creating a positive stroke economy is liberating. Seeing the source of our resistance and inertia is power-giving. The list goes on.

Self-directed behavior change can be delineated pretty clearly. Often it begins with the rejection of a new idea. "It can't possibly be true that human health is directly influenced by physical contact with others." Because such an idea doesn't fit into our belief system, makes us uncomfortable, and portends something we are suspicious of, we deny it. If the advocate is compelling, or the idea is repeated enough, our resistance is lowered and we may tentatively accept the idea. "Maybe there's something to be said for it." As understanding grows, so does agreement and we may make a provisional try at new behavior. If it works, there is confirmation and encouragement to continue.

In the process, setbacks are inevitable. The idea may be lost and forgotten several times. People may find themselves repeatedly having to choose in favor of or against the idea. If there is a succession of affirmative answers along with reinforcing experiences, the new idea and its related behavior will be stabilized in the personality. This process occurs many times in a development program.

THE IMPORTANCE OF INTENTION

As an organization moves from old style to new, a number of changes in policy, work systems, and structure may be undertaken. However, developing people—more precisely, creating the opportunity for workers to develop themselves—is the bottom line. It is important that workers become aware of their ability to create context. Stuck in their positions, they erroneously believe they *are* their belief systems. A breakthrough takes place when they discover they are greater than their point of view.

Historically, the worker's typical point of view is: "I don't count and I don't care." This is a powerless position. One who is stuck there lives his life at survival level. His vision and options are limited to the circumstances of his life. Lamenting the conditions of his life, he sees himself as "caused" by people and forces about him. Coming from the position: "I don't count and I don't care," seeing himself at the effect of his circumstances, he finds himself caught in a downward spiral into ever tighter circles of hopelessness.

Whatever their past experiences, workers have the power to create a new context of "I count and I care." It's a matter of decision. While the old context is derived from childhood, the new is the result of conscious understanding and rational choice. The new returns power to the individual, frees him from his point of view, and returns him to the growth side of the ledger. Steering his own ship, he can now see and experience things as they are.

The basic change takes place when the worker decides "I count and I care" and takes responsibility for himself to create a fresh working reality. Once a new context is chosen, he starts to implement new purpose, goals, and behavior. When a decision is made to create a fresh context, something changes. A new beginning is made. A new situation emerges. This new environment of attitude and action is the fertile soil out of which the worker's sense of self is continually nourished and expanded. The new context empowers the worker's sense of "can do." "I am important." "I can make a difference."

Early confirmation of the power of the new-style context

comes with the discovery that things—all things—work better for him. He accomplishes more with less effort and less stress. He finds himself in flow with work and with the pace of the shop. His life makes more sense. He sees things differently. Bonding with co-workers becomes a source of satisfaction. Although the "I count and I care" decision is solitary and personal, it impacts on everybody. Whatever each of us does makes a difference to all of us. The worker experiences himself having new and positive influence on co-workers, who appear to be drawn into his orbit. They respond to his new "space" with candor and openness. Relationships take on depth and color.

Few disagree with the goal of new-style management to empower workers at all levels. However, each manager or worker will have to make the decision for himself to create and support a new context. At some point comes the solitary moment of the first decision when he goes inside himself to wonder, take stock, and assess which side he will come down on. Once the decision is made, he emerges to set fresh emotional values, expand goals, and try new behavior and attitudes. On some days he will be surprised at how sensible the world is and with what ease he is able to meet his goals. On other days he may repeatedly find himself enmeshed in old-style process and behavior. On those days he will have the opportunity again and again to decide for his new-style context.

"I count and I care" decisions are expressive of the individual's commitment to his best self. They are the outward sign of his intention to create and participate with others in lifting up a whole new array of options, opportunities, and outcomes for work life. Something in the world shifts when a worker comes from the place: "I intend new things for work life." Such intention works to make things happen. It has the power to reify ideas, to give them legs. What before was only propositional or conceptional, under the influence of intention becomes alive, able to walk about and influence others. Good ideas are among the most valuable things we exchange. The new context evokes an inner potential for growth and change. Intention also includes a clear idea of the final outcome the individual desires. Holding onto goals clearly creates an agenda for the mind and makes it possible to make choices that are consistent with the desired end. When one proposes with resolution, energy is focused and directed toward accomplishment. Pursuing deeply held ideas is not always pleasurable. However, it allows of the possibility of greatness. Being conscious of or intending a particular outcome points beyond the self to problems in the environment. The resolution of these may move the human endeavor forward. Intention is powerful stuff.

Organizational change proceeds upon enlisting increasing numbers of workers in alignment with new-style management. By daily deciding and re-deciding for themselves plus enlisting others, the boundaries of consciousness are constantly expanded. Change takes time, but most of all it takes intention.

There are always some people who approve and agree with new style, but nothing happens. That's because they do not make it a matter of intention. They experience no change, no success. Intention empowers the process of change. Sharing one's learnings openly and working hard to accomplish company goals is the way technological society will advance. This is not a moral or ethical position. It is what's so.

5

Team Building

An organization does its work through teams of different kinds. Teams may be "family" groups, such as bosses and subordinates. They may be colleague or peer groups, such as all the regional sales managers or all the division directors of an agency. They may be technical teams, such as the personnel function or quality control. They may be work teams centered around one supervisor. They may be project teams, with members brought together for some specific activity. They may be start-up teams in new enterprises. They may be top management or the board of directors. All organizationwide planned-change efforts have, as one of their early targets, the improvement of team effectiveness. A number of activities can help teams do this.

Following the development model, improvement efforts first focus on the "task" of the team, usually on goal setting, decision making, problem solving, and action planning. Second, work is done on the "processes" of the team, such as the development of the team's working relationships or level of mutual support. Third, training is given on the sources and consequences of member behavior. Fourth, motivations and assumptions below workers' level of awareness are considered.

Team building is useful when new teams are created. Perhaps a new organizational unit is being developed, or a project team is being created, or a temporary system or task force has been put together, or there has been a change in the leadership of a team. New teams often have these characteristics:

Confusion as to roles and relationships.
Fairly clear understanding of short-term goals.
Technical competence—the attribute which puts members on the team.
Team leaders who focus on the task rather than on process and behavior.

Experience indicates that if team activities initially focus on task and work problems, relationship problems soon develop, as they do in any human system. There is considerable payoff if a new team can first examine how it is going to work together, what its methods, procedures, and work relationships will be, and what the priority concerns of its members are. Such a team will work more effectively, have fewer interpersonal problems, and be more productive and meaningful to its members.

One design that has been effective in a number of new team development efforts involves a two-day meeting away from the work site. The meeting is scheduled during the early weeks of the team's life. The form varies, but the following components are usually included:

1. Statement, discussion, and clarification of the mission of the group, including its goals, timetable, and work assignments.
2. Presentation and explanation of the leader's plan to organize work, the group's relationship to other parts of the system, and ground rules. This is a good time for the leader to share information on his or her administrative style and practices.
3. Discussion of the concerns and hopes of group members. Members of new groups frequently are concerned about their roles, their relationship to the leader, whether the

group will stay with or depart from tradition, the reward system, and what will happen to them when the task is ended. Early clarification of these matters can make a significant difference in productivity.

4. Discussion of the major areas of responsibility and authority of each member. Members are given an opportunity to describe what they see as their function and responsibilities. They check their perceptions with the leader and with other team members.

5. Development of mechanisms for communications within the team—such as staff meetings, memoranda, task forces, and subprojects. When appropriate, plans are set for inducting the rest of the organization into the program.

6. Arrangement for follow-up meetings. This is an important step, particularly if the group is to continue working over an extended period.

When the new team is created because of a change in leadership, the leader should at the outset define his or her expectations, style, goals, and aspirations, and request feedback from members on how these fit their expectations and aspirations. Collaborative goal-setting efforts at the beginning of the new leader's term significantly reduce the loss of productivity that usually follows change of leadership.

TEAM-BUILDING MODELS

Three models have proved successful for working with family teams. The first type uses interviews, feedback, and action planning. A consultant (or other resource outside the team) interviews members a day or so before the meeting. The consultant asks each member two questions: "What can be done to increase the effectiveness of the operations of the team, and of the organization? What are the obstacles to achieving this?" Results of the interviews are tabulated and categorized under major headings. The meeting begins with the consultant feeding back information collected from the team members. The first task of the group is to go through the data and build an agenda for action.

The major activity in such a meeting is problem solving. The group solves those problems for which it has the resources and develops mechanisms for handling items that have to be forwarded to some other part of the organization. At the end of the meeting the team has an action plan plus a timetable. This development activity may focus on improving the work of the team, setting goals, improving the relationships of team members, or all three. It is determined in large part by the nature of the problems brought up during the interviews.

Another form of team building is based on training workers in such areas as communication skills, management by objectives, and decision making. An educational seminar is held to teach group members needed behavioral concepts and skills. Members then meet to plan improvement of their own organization, using instruments learned in the educational part of the program. When training has an action orientation, it is a form of team building.

Another model utilizes an unstructured group. A team goes off site to a "laboratory" for two or three days to work without an agenda. It is called a laboratory because participants learn from the behavior generated at the meeting. They examine it, generalize from it, and apply it to the work setting. This model focuses heavily on interpersonal relationships and team processes. It gives secondary emphasis to problem solving, action planning, and connecting learning to tasks.

One other form of team building that occurs frequently in large organizations is the professional team meeting. People performing the same work in different locations come together to exchange information and ideas and to develop stronger membership in their own profession. The format focuses on collecting information before the meeting to develop an agenda.

Below we consider the total team-building process under the following headings:

Contracting
Data collection
Use of the development model
Consulting strategies
Reaching critical mass
Methodologies
Closure

CONTRACTING

I have had mediocre success in selling development programs. Approaching a company cold does not work well for me. Companies sell themselves and seek assistance. The skill is to convert their interest into a workable contract. Usually, as a prerequisite to undertaking a new-style development program the company must have real and immediate business problems it wants solved. A large number of business failures are in the "will do," not the "can do," area. Often the former must be resolved before something can be done on the latter. Typical problems I have encountered in being asked to work with a team include:

Integration of a recently purchased company.
Restructuring of a sales organization.
Control of spiraling costs.
Breakdown of communications into destructive fighting.
Where to place a new manufacturing facility.
How to reduce losses through error.
Getting an R&D effort back on track.

Corrosive labor-management relations.
Decision to install management by objectives.
Need to reduce turnover among first-line managers.
Decision to build a new management team.
Shrinking the workforce by a third.
Moving to a plant 200 miles away.

Sometimes I am asked to do things I am unable or unwilling to do. I do not undertake programs when there is a strong likelihood of failure. Refusals include the following.

1. An assembly plant asked us to "infiltrate" the ranks of the plant shop to identify troublemakers. The company wanted forewarning about possible wildcat strikes. When we countered with a team-building proposal, management expressed amazement that we should "want to solve the problem."

2. An airline official asked us to turn his department around. His job was on the line. The situation had deteriorated to the point that people were solidified in their positions and no longer accessible to reason.

3. A division head was distressed by the crazy behavior among those who reported to him. When we reported his contribution to the misbehavior and he discovered that he himself would have to change, he decided it would be less troublesome to live with the craziness of others.

4. A manufacturer wanted us to use the latest behavioral science to evaluate the workforce and "separate the good apples from the bad." It is not within the nature of a development contract to evaluate people in a way they don't understand and can't influence.

To be successful, a development program must follow three critical guidelines. The first is "No mystery." Openness on business issues is essential within the organization. Secrecy and old style are synonymous and therein is great potential for organizational mischief, games, and politics. At times, of course, it is inappropriate to discuss proprietary, legal, marketing, engineering, and financial matters, but the need for such restraint should be handled openly. Some companies find this hard to deal with. There are things they prefer to keep hidden. Except in unusual circumstances, secrecy is counterproductive. No mystery also means that the theory, intentions, and goals of the program will be explained to all employees. Any questions about the program, member behavior, issues, and objectives will be answered. Tactics and processes are shared and are open to testing and correction. No information is withheld from members that is not destructive. The goal is "to tell the truth and support people."

The second rule in any development program is "No games or politics." Sometimes those in control desire to solidify their position and attitudes. Those on the outs hope for new power. A development program is not geared to any one party. It seeks to create new conditions of openness and trust so parties can solve the business disputes between them. Sometimes both parties to the dispute resist change because without their games and politics they would have to face real issues. Better the noise and confusion of ritual fight.

Change threatens power. The first task of those responsible for a development program is to assess the readiness of the senior group to change. It is not good to accept for others what they are not willing to accept for themselves. The ability to skillfully confront those in control is fundamental to a successful program. Usually no one else can or wants to do it. Many times, those in senior places are there for good reason. Their concern and their competence are genuine. The following guidelines are essential when contracting with a company:

1. Contract clearly. Make sure Parent, Adult, and Child of both parties agree.
2. Call all duplex transactions. Openly discuss people's attitudes about process and behavior.
3. Practice good nurturing skills.

4. Don't get too far ahead of the organization.
5. Confront with caring.

The third rule of a development program is "No rescuing." The role of doctor is very seductive. Giving instant "cures" is an age-old strategy. It is a powerful stroke. It gives benefits to both parties. The norm of "no rescuing" obligates those responsible for a development program not to solve others' problems. Their task is to help others get their hands on their own problems and resolve them. Then the company is well served and work becomes a source of growth, recognition, and achievement.

DATA COLLECTION

Interviewing is the primary technique for collecting data on how the organization works, at both the corporate and the individual level. From interviews, a composite picture of company dynamics can be created. Out of this composite, entitled "old style," will arise development goals (desired state) and implementing strategies. These goals and processes, entitled "new style," will be the measure of the program's success.

Companies usually solicit help when the unit is not producing adequately and no longer responds to traditional management controls. When an organization malfunctions, it is hard to influence. It often exhibits one or more of the following symptoms:

1. Rumor abounds, with high levels of distortion.
2. Tension is high; members experience rising levels of stress.
3. Behavior is political, gamey, and defensive.
4. Thinking tends to be convergent at the expense of individual judgment.
5. The long view is sacrificed for quick solutions.

Good interview skills—creating a friendly atmosphere, withholding judgment, encouraging discharge, and using feedback liberally—will make the initial intervention into the system a positive step forward.

A secondary purpose of interviewing is to secure the interviewee's alignment with the program. Those who have survived under an authority-obedient system for many years often are buoyed by the prospect of liberation from past abuse, the opportunity to solve work problems, and the chance to gain some influence over how things are done in the shop. A few will view the concern for improving the quality of work life with suspicion, on the grounds that it is "too far-fetched" or that management's intentions are not genuine.

The sincerity of management's commitment should be assured before initiating interviews. Each employee should be encouraged to accept responsibility for his or her behavior during interviews. If employees have any reasonable suspicion, they should not leave themselves unprotected. Program goals are made clear to enlist their support and participation. At the same time, they should not surrender responsibility for their behavior.

Each interview is an opportunity to make the objectives of the program known. Below are some major themes that the interviewer should present. Time constraints will govern the amount of time spent on each.

1. Old- and new-style organizational values and behaviors differ significantly. The importance of openness, collaboration, mutual interdependence, and responsibility should be pointed out.
2. Those responsible for the development program are committed not to participate in games, politics, rescuing, or mystery.
3. Employees will not be evaluated to management in a way

they don't know about or in a way that does them a disservice.

4. The target of the program is the entire organization. The goal is to improve its ability to compete more effectively in the marketplace.

Provision for feedback is an important part of interviewing. It is an abuse of employees to collect information from them and then not report on conclusions and findings. Fundamental to bringing about transformation is the inclusion of as many people as possible at all stages of the program. Whereas old-style managers accepted secrecy as the norm, new-style managers begin early to demonstrate the motivational value of openness. Dyed-in-the-wool old-stylers will say it can't be done. Experience proves them wrong. There are very few matters employees can't be trusted with, including wage ranges and benefits.

The theme of new style is: "You can ask us about any business issue at any time. We will talk about anything." The contract looks like this:

We will discuss with you any business issue you ask about. Or we will tell you why we won't and when and under what conditions we will.

Openness has important motivational value for employees. They feel part of the real organization and can understand its problems and their responsibility for them. This sense of responsibility for levels above, below, and parallel to one's own supports a heightened sense of self-worth and ownership of company problems.

Do not collect heavy data during the interviews. Don't dig for possibly questionable activities. These matters, if they influence business, will surface later when the organization will be in a better position to work on them. If you get dirt, you're stuck with it. It isn't helpful and tends to promote games and politics. What is needed is an assessment of what employees seek to improve in themselves and what they see as useful to increase unit cost-effectiveness.

If inertia is high, set up "serial interviews"—that is, more than one with the same manager. A few managers will resist interviewing. After several interviews, it is not hard to discover where their defensiveness is coming from and what they are protecting. Do not try to overcome or end-run defensiveness. Your task is to create an opportunity for the employee to take charge of his or her own growth. Often rigidity is but another example of an old-style manager who, when in trouble, does more of what created the problem in the first place.

Since note taking may cause anxiety for the interviewee, you might omit it until after the interview. If you prefer to take notes, the following contract can be offered:

> I am going to make notes here for my own benefit. They will be useful later on when we come to planning the change program. They will help me recall your concerns and needs. At the end of the interview, I will let you read my notes. I welcome corrections and additions and am willing to give you a photocopy.

Most managers waive the opportunity to read the notes. Some scan them casually or read about critical incidents. A few will read them carefully and suggest corrections. Some will ask about when and how they will receive the report. Rarely will anyone request photocopies.

Several major benefits flow to employees from the interviewing process. As researcher, you are responsible for making sure these happen.

1. Employees have an opportunity to enjoy a nurturing experience. While this may be new and initially upsetting to them, they will go away feeling better about themselves, their work, and the program.

2. The vast majority of organizational problems have their roots in the past. Before these problems can be resolved, de-

structure processes must be turned around, old hurts discharged, and work restructured. The researcher creates a safe situation that allows the employee to ventilate past frustration, consternation, and pain. It is a significant event in the worker's life to report "war stories" of battles lost with company style and obdurate employer attitudes. The report is often accompanied by rising tones, palm smacking, purple language, and a sense of incredulousness. If the employee is allowed to discharge feelings, they will disappear and will no longer be available to debilitate the employee and the unit process.

The interviewer's task is to encourage full discharge of feelings. Such material need only be accepted. Most of it needs no attention. It is usually long past and outside the influence of contemporary events. Ancient slights and hurts not discharged can operate today with the same emotional energy they had many years ago. No interviewer can help wondering at the unnecessary emotional loads employees are forced to carry around. When an employee is able to fully discharge his or her feelings, they disappear.

3. Employees anticipate good things for themselves out of the development program. Each employee plans his or her own benefits. In each unit the character of the members and their readiness to change and accept responsibility largely govern what beneficial outcomes they will enjoy.

The interviews should focus primarily on problems with production and processes. Questions directed at behavioral and motivational levels come later. Substantive topics covered may include the following:

1. Unit production, quality, technological competence, and ability to make timely deliveries.
2. Financial reporting on areas of cost, gross, and net margins.
3. Labor-management relations, bargaining history with unions, and grievance-arbitration record.

4. Wage and salary program, including the benefits package. Is it internally equitable and externally competitive?
5. Work structuring, plus materials and maintenance handling.
6. The role of research and development.

The development model can help you organize your interviewing technique. Below are suggested questions to elicit key data. Make sure your questions are open and not leading. Rephrase them to serve your needs.

Company Level

What level of profitability have senior managers achieved over the past few years?

How do they set unit goals?

What is their style of operation?

What is the best way to influence them?

Can they be counted on to act in the best interest of the company?

Who are pivotal members of the company and what are the key relationships?

Team or Unit Level

What is the level of trust?

Are unit goals clear to you?

What is the style of operation?

How are decisions made?

What is the price of membership in the organization (inclusion issues)?

Who has the power and how is it used (control issues)?

How much energy do members commit to the task and how productive are they (production issues)?

How are differences dealt with in team?

Do members understand and manage process?

Are matters of concern brought to the surface and faced with candor?

Are communications natural and easy or diminished and distorted?

What is the quality of thinking applied to problems?

Are training activities supported?

Two-Person Level

How much does A trust B?

Can A confront B with caring?

Is A overfriendly with B?

Is the chemistry bad between A and B?

Is A or B overly protective of C?

What is their fight style?

Can they discuss their relationship openly and not collect bad feelings?

Do they exhibit mutual bad feelings?

Do they exhibit mutual support and interdependence?

Individual Employee Level

What is the employee's field and level of competence?

How much Adult is available?

What is the relative strength of Parent, Adult, and Child ego states?

How open is the employee to other views of his or her behavior?

What is the contamination level of the Adult? How open is it?

Is the full spectrum of feelings available and appropriate?

How clear and operative are the employee's values?

Can the employee support intimacy and direct encounters?

Can the employee interrupt games?

Motivational Level

Does the employee see himself (or herself) causing his own behavior, or does he blame it on others?

Can the employee distinguish his or her agenda from that of others?

Does the employee understand projection?

What is the employee's frequency of craziness (behavior not under rational control)?

Is "reachback" present (future events influencing today's behavior)?

Is "afterburn" present (past events continuing to influence today's activities)?

The issues above are extensive and are listed only as suggestions to guide your efforts. Successful research techniques nurture employees, give them maximum opportunity to fully discharge, and enlist their responsible downstream participation in the development program.

USE OF THE DEVELOPMENT MODEL

The development model represents four levels in training managers and workers to bring process and behavior under control:

1. It represents the order in which problems are faced and resolved.
2. It demonstrates the layering of problems and helps reduce communications confusion.
3. It is a training device that sensitizes managers and workers to process and behavior.
4. It helps establish a time frame of activities for the development program.

As noted earlier, there are four levels in the model: problem solving, process management, behavior training, and motivational activities. Process is dealt with by members only when it causes problem solving to slow down or stop. Behavior training is undertaken only when member behavior corrodes the process and makes it hard for the group to function. Usually the training is limited to what the members need at the moment. Motivational activities are undertaken when behavior must be strengthened to get back to problem solving.

CONSULTING STRATEGIES

At times everyone feels the need for help and attempts to give help. The cardinal principle is: "Help is never really helpful unless it is perceived as helpful by the recipient." Anything else is "helping the hell out of somebody." Everyone at some time is a consultant. Consultation is a personal relationship between a person (or organization) who is trying to solve a problem and a person (or group) who is offering assistance in these efforts. The consultant's task is to help the client:

1. See the situation objectively in a new and fresh way.
2. Consider other options to the present course or other solutions to problems.
3. Discover and use all available resources.
4. Develop worker potential.

An effective consulting relationship requires a sharing of knowledge, attitudes, and skills related to problem solving, process, and behavior management. The relationship is voluntary, temporary, and based on shared assumptions. It is supportive of company goals and standards. Several phases are involved.

1. *Training.* From their broad base in the problem area and enriched experience, the consultants (internal or external) supply the knowledge and insight necessary to create new directions for the organization. Often very little of what a consultant brings is new. Part of the consultative dilemma is to turn the "political" information provided by a member into useful information.

2. *Enlisting others.* After the purpose of the program has been agreed on and goals and strategies set, others must be aligned to the new style. The goal is to enlarge the ranks of those who are willing to tell the truth, take responsibility for their work, and try new behavior. When a majority of members are enlisted in the new-style process, the consciousness of all is influenced and eventually the organization is transformed.

3. *Intrusion.* When key members or sections of the company rebel, confrontation is essential. The problem must be uncovered and dealt with. When behavior is defensive, disruptive, and low on energy or momentum, intrusion may be called for. Energy is focused on the resistant part of the system to confront its process and member behavior. The attempt is to hook members' Adult and free their Natural Child. Confronting these people in a caring way may be the hardest thing we are called upon to do.

4. *Counseling.* From time to time counseling with parts of the organization or key members is necessary. Since the task is to assist members in becoming resources for one another's problems, counseling may be largely modeling. This is known as "corridor work." It is usually a side discussion parallel to the main effort. The major task is to create opportunities for workers to work together to solve their problems.

5. *Withdrawing.* Allowing workers to risk new behavior, fail, and learn is an important part of the development process. Many managers have admitted that one of the hardest things for them to do is allow subordinates to fail. It's so tempting to interrupt workers' efforts and set them straight. Failure is an important part of learning how to use available resources. Learning takes place at both the emotional and the cognitive level. Neither one should be denied to workers. The temporary nature of the consulting relationship should always be kept in mind by both parties.

REACHING CRITICAL MASS

As the program develops, larger numbers of workers accept responsibility for their work problems, process, and behavior. What started out as change, if extended far enough, becomes transformation. New attitudes of openness and cooperation create a corporate "can do" spirit that leads to improvements in creativity, work quality, and productivity.

Before the program, managers and workers do business as they always have. They are initially resistant to the program, as they are to any change. As inertia is overcome, change takes place among a few and spreads to others. The rate of change within the organization accelerates. When a majority of the members accept responsibility for process and behavior and internalize the management of change, "critical mass" is reached and the organization is transformed. Rather than resisting change, the system has internalized a process for dealing with it. Rather than fearing future challenges, the system welcomes them as an opportunity for greater success. Workers operate in a new context where they are the cause of change instead of the effect. No social problem is beyond their concern.

The following are signs that an organization is approaching or has reached critical mass:

1. The group has a high sense of self-awareness along with pride in membership. Ownership of the company mission, strategies, and tactics is real at all levels.
2. All business indicators show significant improvement.
3. There is an absence of games and a marked reduction in politics—replaced by a realistic awareness of work issues.
4. In meetings, the collective effort of group members is more powerful than the sum total of individual inputs.
5. Great energy is released into the system and is available for work.
6. Workers support and nurture one another easily and naturally. People welcome being cared for.

7. Process and behavior are under active management and workers make and share discoveries for themselves.

METHODOLOGIES

The development program can take a variety of forms. Since the overriding task is to solve business problems, the strategies selected will be determined by the problems revealed in the diagnosis. The following are common elements of programs:

1. *Team building.* Group problems are surveyed and resolved and action is planned.

2. *Management training.* While this may occur at all levels, at the first-line level it is most important. You can't overtrain supervision.

3. *Floor meetings with workers.* Regularly scheduled meetings are held with hourly rated employees to discuss quality of work.

4. *Labor-management relations.* Although labor and management have retained their traditional responsibilities and maintained their arm's-length relationship, they are finding an increasing number of ways in which cooperation serves their best interests.

5. *Wage and salary administration.* Because many organizations have not established internal equity and external competitiveness in their salary programs, this may be an important part of a development effort. Performance appraisal can be dealt with under this heading or handled separately.

6. *Management by objectives.* This is a strategy of working with the total organization to clarify purposes and goals. Either one can be the basis of a new-style development program.

7. *Sales training.* Retail organizations have experienced real improvement in both structure and function when members are trained in process and behavior management. They

have found team building a great way to heighten consciousness and release energy for work.

8. *Special problems.* From time to time special problems call for concentrated effort and skill. Consider the following: purchasing a company and integrating it with the parent; dealing with the takeover of a warehouse by an armed revolutionary force; and coping with rapidly deteriorating market conditions or the cutoff of a supply of raw materials. Unusual circumstances call for unusual effort, through which new-style companies can show off their flexibility, intelligence, and power.

CLOSURE

Terminating a relationship puts stress on both parties. Whether the consultants are internal or external, separation from a group creates feelings of loss on both sides. In a development program, important things happen to people. Mastering stress, winning with new behavior, working in a positive environment, enjoying problem solving—all these things transform people.

All development programs should include a discussion of closure at the outset so that neither part builds a dependency relationship. Part of being effective in a technological society involves meeting, quickly building a working relationship, and splitting. Learning to bring about completion and separation is a new-style skill. I have experienced a variety of closures working with organizations. Here are five different conclusions to a consulting relationship I have seen.

1. *Completion.* If goals are clear and the time frame is limited, completion can be obtained. In a training program, when concrete materials are delivered to workers over a given time span and the results can be tested, a company can experience both success and closure.

Key results include an improvement of regular business

indicators—productivity, quality, and work methods—plus a reduction of scrap loss, grievances, and absenteeism. On the process level, the goal is to create a high-energy climate with openness and effective team problem solving. On the behavioral level, the presence of spontaneity, authenticity, and intuition are most prized. On the motivational level, playing the game 100 percent is the prize.

2. *Fatigue.* Infrequently projects end because one or both parties no longer have the energy or interest to pursue them. Development interventions are powerful because change can be immediate and visible. Programs tend to grow by including others who want to participate and experience for themselves an enhanced sense of power. When there is a loss of energy, money, or insight, or when the program no longer meets people's needs, ennui may set in. A sign that this is happening occurs when the program starts belonging to the consultant and not the company. Low energy is a key indicator of organizational malaise.

3. *Resignation.* In a couple of instances the consultant may be asked to take part in activities of doubtful legal or ethical standing. A good policy in cases of this sort is to discuss the problem openly with the management team, with the expectation that the matter will be corrected. On one occasion I was asked to penetrate a section of 70 workers where there was great discontent. The company wanted to identify group leaders and receive advance notice of impending trouble. When it became clear this was the only level of problem solving that management cared about, I demurred. In another instance I stumbled on a double set of books. When I revealed this, management expressed astonishment and ended the practice.

4. *Defeat.* Is there anyone who hasn't had to learn how to deal with failure? Sometimes you can only walk away from a situation and ponder, "What went wrong?" Defeat is the necessary path to maturity, and there are no shortcuts.

5. *Transition.* There comes a time when the consultant has

done everything possible for a company. A plateau is reached and it is in the best interests of the organization to get the fresh view of a newcomer. One of the difficulties of being an internal consultant is that you tend to become socialized to your own system. The need for acceptance may dull the cutting edge of your perception. The same need may also make it difficult for you to challenge work teams that have become too accustomed to mediocrity. The external consultant, too, may have to withdraw so the organization gets a fresh grip on its problems.

Management's purpose in a development program is to make its power available to employees so they can collectively manage the company environment. Some call this the humanization of industry. Giving employees greater influence over company behavior and business problems is consistent with what contemporary management research says employees want. It corresponds to union rhetoric and to what workers themselves say they desire. Employees seek more influence over their work.

Experience teaches us, however, that increased power is not always met with cheers of liberation and joy. It is sobering to realize that greater power involves workers more deeply in relationships with others. It does not distance them from human turmoil. Paradoxically, the more status workers have, the less they are able to prosper by their own efforts and the more they are dependent on the efforts of others. Social development comes slowly and demands clear and consistent effort. People grow at different speeds. It is painful for some who respond wholeheartedly to new opportunities to discover inertia, cynicism, and rebellion among their peers. The rationalizations of the obstructionists are myriad: "This is just another management strategy to screw the worker." "You don't believe they'll ever give you anything without a fight, do you?" "Just more time-wasting meetings to take us away from what we're here to do." And the old chestnut: "We shouldn't air our dirty laundry in public. It's better that employees not know the truth. No telling what they'll do."

Few escape the crazies who work in a crazy system. When craziness defines what's going down, then rational people will act crazy. When the system victimizes, all are victims. True, the three manipulative roles—victim, persecutor, and rescuer—shift among members. No one stays on top for long. Soon the persecutor becomes the victim again calling for a rescuer. And so the game goes. A most sobering reality about old-style companies is their predictability. The only relief from the magic show is infrequent small victories, rebellion, sickness, and vacations.

When employees are given more power over their work, their initial confusion, rejection, and anger are understandable. So is the irony of their first response: "Tell us what to do." Workers have so long been part of the rank-and-file that they are often cynical and disbelieving when they are offered a chance to take responsibility. Sometimes employees get excited about their new opportunities and, unable to distinguish between the central and the peripheral, attempt too much too soon. When pent-up ideas held with certainty are discharged into reality, a period of adjustment necessarily follows.

Don't expect gratitude for your efforts. Many workers have been led down the primrose path once too often. Their cynicism may be a sign of healthy self-concern. If you are committed to openness and problem solving, if your behavior supports your intentions, and if you are patient, they'll join you. Expect them to test you. If they have been much abused, the test may be severe. You will have much opportunity to remember your commitment to reason and nurturance.

When I suggest that it may be necessary to use some coercion to bring about improvement, managers sometimes grin and sneer: "I guess your strategies don't always work; maybe you've failed this time." "Do you think it's right," they ask in mocking tones, "to act arbitrarily to fire somebody when you advocate openness and trust?" There are a couple of errors here. Advocating collaboration is not the same thing as making it real. There are likely to be a few people in the system who are too far gone to be retrieved without psychiatric counseling. Some benefit from the old system and don't want it changed. Resistant old-stylers need to be dealt with directly and expeditiously. This always has a positive effect on those who want to try the new. I do not advocate managers giving away power. Collaboration is the best way to use power. If you protect and shelter your power, it drains away. If you share it, it grows. Keep it and lose it. Share it and gain more. Few doubt this common sense.

There is no change without stress. All of us would like things to be orderly and clear. We would like to avoid confusion, ambiguity, tension, and threat. Neatness and antiseptic rationality are not characteristic of company development programs. To overcome inertia, resistance, rebellion, and cynicism, you must remain clear about your assumptions, tactics, and goals. Do this and trust the process. No matter how inappropriate employee responses may seem, in time things will work out. Employees can't drive you to the trenches unless you choose to go.

Some managers see trust building and support behavior as a sign of weakness or loss of vigor. I do not advocate strong people acting weak or bright people tolerating confusion. No behavior is strong or weak in itself. The test is whether the particular behavior furthers company goals. If you're dealing with a Rebellious Child–dominant individual with decommissioned Parent and Adult, you don't have many options. If the employee cannot be reached with your Adult, your next best option is threatening Parent. Such a person might not consider you serious if you come out of some other posture. You may not wish to deploy such behavior, or reinforce it in others, but it may be mandated by the facts. If this is so, it is an act of kindness to invest the amount of anger necessary. Lesser options include ignoring or separating the employee. These, while less attractive, may in certain cases be in the worker's best interest. Behavior management means being clear about where you're coming from, accepting responsibility for the consequences, and acting openly and honestly in the best interests of the company and the employees.

Some people cope with the vagaries of social life by mounting a single behavioral posture. Piety, rationality, and positionality are examples. Some members of the helping professions value speaking quietly or using summary feedback as a total strategy. They support the idea that perpetual kindness is the only effective approach. They reject the less attractive behaviors of the tenacious Adult, the pressuring Parent, and the hyper Child.

Such a monochromatic approach will not work in a development program. When you are responsible for changing an organizational system, you need the flexibility of a variety of approaches. The stance is neither forbearance nor stoicism. Your task is to do what is necessary to get the job done. In this effort, clarity and openness become critical. Being explicit about your goals does much to clarify process. Openness is necessary to maintain integrity. Sharing with others will also keep you afloat amid the shifting waters of the group.

Appropriateness is the issue. Does your behavior support your intentions? You may decide to swim against the stream. This comes to everyone in life if they are goal oriented. Once you understand that integrity means keeping all systems open, dynamic, and productive, it becomes clear: Winning is not everything—unless you don't care about your own integrity, others' survival, or furthering social goals.

Responding appropriately means having your feelings available so you can be tender when the opportunity occurs. It means having an ethical structure you can refer to when problems arise that demand choices favoring some against others. It means having your Adult sufficiently developed so you are able to distinguish between reality and what others have chosen to believe. It means being able to use the approach that fares best in a particular situation.

6

Seven Key Profiles

This chapter discusses seven key managerial profiles I have seen over the years in companies. These, at least, are clear to me. If you were listening to my voice dictate this material, you would hear my attempt to be descriptive, not judgmental. What will interest readers most is the discussion of the social consequences of the several profiles.

I believe behavior can be managed like any business problem. It must first be seen and its regularities discovered. Workers then can consider their own profile and its consequences, make such judgments as may seem appropriate to them, and begin a program of learning by discovery. They may, for instance, attempt more Adult behavior by asking more questions. They may desire more nurturing behavior from others. They may observe the consequences for others of stroke starvation. Such a program of learning can only take place in an organization committed to creating conditions that help workers grow, an organization in which feedback is immediate, directed toward work behavior, and given without judgment.

A basic source for these descriptions is the *PAC Self-Scoring Scales,* a useful instrument for measuring the relative strength of ego states. In addition, I have spent thousands of hours in participant observation of work groups at every level in a wide variety of corporations.

In some ways the most fruitful source for the profiles is the personal testimony of those who have taken responsibility for their own behavior and stopped assuming it to be caused by factors outside themselves. I don't refer here to "think about" or "talk about." These after-the-fact explanations lack immediacy and authenticity and often have the sound of someone defending against attack. Such defendants do not understand the emotional foundation of behavior. They erroneously assume thought precedes action, which issues in feeling. In fact, almost all behavior is emotionally based. Afterward thinking comes along as a sort of add-on with its explanations and justifications. You will never get far listening to "think about" or "talk about." Since the right order is feeling, doing, and thinking, to get at the heart of behavior you must discover its feeling component. When this is reported it has the unmistakable ring of authenticity. It sounds true. Listeners feel they're getting the real thing. Of course, when you have all three together, you feel confident that you have isolated a genuine type.

Delineating a particular type of personality does not imply purity or singularity. Part of the meaning of "human elegance" is that behavior has vast and complex motivational sources. Indeed, our strategy is to aid workers in mobilizing a larger portion of this sizable resource. Oversimplifying by reduction of ambiguity, denial of complexity, or selective thinking is counterproductive. Companies need all the rational-affect-moral power they can muster. They need to mobilize all that is available to them. It is useful and totally accurate to see behavior as the functioning of a dynamic mechanism whose regularities can be understood and can be influenced by the self and others. Life is paradoxical. Behavior is at the same time incredibly elegant and blindingly simple. These two truths are repeatedly forced on us.

Behavior can successfully be understood and dealt with on the expressed level. We can also by inference discuss the amount of energy, spirit, or "power" an individual invests in each of the three ego states. Human behavior, though dynamic, is limited. This means the amount of energy available to invest in ego states is a given. Besides the amount of energy available for ego states, there are levels of awareness and control as well as degrees of resistance to moving across ego state boundaries. Combining these three—amount of energy invested, level of rational control, and ease of movement across boundaries—I have observed the following scale of ego state investment among workers:

2.00 *Dominance.* Usually only one ego state is available for use. The other two may be badly decommissioned or even excluded. Decommissioned means the ego state is underdeveloped and does not have enough power to make itself felt. This is usually caused by inadequate rearing practices.

1.00 *Intermittent contamination of adult.* This occurs when the Adult has insufficient power to take responsibility for the individual's behavior. It is overwhelmed by incursions from overdeveloped Parent and Child. These weaken its effective control so that behavior is erratic, unpredictable, and often inappropriate. The Adult, of course, is incipiently the most powerful ego state. When properly developed, it has no fear of being overwhelmed by the other two. The first step in strengthening personal responsibility is seeing this. The Adult has the self-confirming ability to achieve here-and-now awareness and to see things as they really are, as opposed to how others taught us to see them. When we have experienced this sense of self, we are transformed. We need not ever again fear losing control to the destructive Parent or distracting Child.

0.00 *Appropriate functioning.* Each ego state is fully developed and available for use at the appropriate time and place. Besides being able to shape effective responses to the environment, people who function at this level can try new behavior and attempt innovative social arrangements. They can live their lives "at cause." Themselves as the primary resource, they interact with all elements of a social system and work to create something new and fresh.

0.01 *Intermittent decommission.* One, several, or all ego states may suffer from malnutrition. The person simply does not have enough energy to make all the machinery function at an effective level. At this level behavior is energized below the point necessary for successful effort. The ill-defined Parent exhibits drifting and waffling behavior. The weakened Adult does not accept responsibility for the personality and denies the necessity of self-discipline. The enfeebled Child is "tuned out" and passive.

0.02 *Excluded.* If one ego state is not available for use, its absence may not be immediately obvious. For example, the Parent and Adult can work together to represent a passable Child, the Parent and Child can cooperate so the excluded Adult is not visible. However, over time and under pressure of adverse circumstances, the absent ego state will become clear. The consequences are often critical. Third-degree games (ones that involve physical harm) are indulged in all too frequently, sickness may be chronic, self-fulfilling prophecy is visible, and craziness abounds.

In Table 2 the scale of energy investment is the dependent variable and the three ego states the independent variable. The cells report some characteristics of members of each group. The table suggests some interrelationships between the three ego states.

PROFILE I

(P) LOW PARENT

(A) HIGH ADULT

(C) HIGH NATURAL CHILD

This is the person whose OK Child has permission to be close to people, who trusts and believes in the new and fresh. The Child adds warmth, intuition, and creativity to deliberations of the Adult. This is the most effective manager. When the Punishing Parent is minimal and values are mediated through the Adult, the Adult-Child relationship is enhanced.

A senior finance officer of a large consumer products corporation comes to mind as a good example. Brad was an unfailingly friendly person. His decisions about employees were based more on gut hunches than on company politics, psychology, or stereotypes. If he "felt" good about you, as he did about most people, he listened carefully, took a position, and kept his agreements. Several things about his behavior were characteristic. He was thorough in preparation and a careful planner. He tended to bring people together around complex issues and to work toward consensus. His intellectual clarity and his friendliness made him a favorite up and down the line.

Brad always withheld negative judgments. His Adult would temper his critical Parent as he carefully searched for the words to describe an employee who was not working up to capabilities. He discussed disagreements with others carefully and deliberately. The self-policing of his Adult made him comfortable to work with—or to disagree with.

Before hiring Brad, the company found itself in a deteriorating relationship with a large, militant union that represented 70 percent of the workforce. Employee cynicism and resistance were expressed in absenteeism, grievances, vitriolic bargaining, poor productivity, and strikes. Because the rank-and-file came to trust him, Brad became an important link between union and management—a relationship he labored to improve. He committed himself to maintaining the legitimate interests of both parties. I can hear him now: "Labor relations need not be a win-lose or lose-lose game. Two things are important— never give up your integrity and never win too big." This attitude was refreshing in a company that previously had justified lying on the grounds "Winning isn't everything, it's the only thing." Many times Brad found himself in the unenviable position of trying to influence both sides to take a moderate stand.

As he faced negotiations one year, Brad decided it was time to improve the bargaining climate. If both parties better un-

Table 2. Characteristics of the three ego states.

Scale	Parent	Adult	Child
2.00 **Dominance** (Usually only one state available)	Domineering Treats people as awkward children Fosters dependency Judgmental Hardworking Moralistic Perpetual rescuer Closed to new ideas Desires unlimited power	Has difficulty working with others Oriented to objects and facts Unfeeling, sterile relationships Risk-avoiding Uninvolved Unable to emphathize	Can't think; short span of attention Perpetual little boy or girl Wants to be taken care of Seeks out a Parent who will applaud, punish, reward, "baby" Likes routine with no responsibility
1.00 **Intermittent** **Contamination** **of Adult** (Control is erratic or expression inappropriate)	Areas of prejudice held; not open to new data Accepts slogans Discounting Opinionated	Unfeeling or overrriding Repetitious, boring behavior Unsympathetic behavior Periodic loss of control	Fantasy Distorted perception of reality Unable to make decisions and stay with them Projections Lacks definition Blames others

Table 2. (continued)

Scale	Parent	Adult	Child
0.00 **Appropriate** **Functioning** (Each state is fully developed and available for appropriate use)	Rationally held positions about race, religion, nationalism, social arrangements, and sex Knows history Firmly and agreeably structured	Grounded in present reality Clarifies assumptions and estimates probabilities High tolerance for ambiguity, paradox, and irony Growth-oriented	Full spectrum of feelings available and expressed Lives passionately Spontaneity, creativity, and intuition are important dynamics Enjoys intimacy, touching, animals, and nature
0.01 **Intermittent** **Decommission** (Low energy investment; ego states periodically ineffective)	Areas of weak self-definition Often unable to take a stand with conviction and feeling Waffling and drifting behavior may be prominent Weak in history Can be led into unethical or illegal behavior	Areas of Adult contamination by Parent or Child Understanding of own and others' behavior is weak May have difficulty contacting others Intelligence is limited by absence of discipline and training	Limited affect competence Discomfort with softer feelings Feelings available usually only around Parent concerns May be tuned out and passive Weak transactions Sentimentality
0.02 **Excluded** (Little or no energy; ego states available only in unusual circumstances)	Confusion about place of self in social context No clear idea of right and wrong Cynicism about social life Identity loss No operable ethical position Estranged from others	Blocked-out Adult leads to pathological behavior Behavior patterns deteriorate toward destruction of self and others Chronic behavior Disturbed	Functions with excluded Child as a robot, computer, technocrat No warmth Big on rationalization, defensiveness, and explanation Denial important Sterile and boring

derstood and trusted each other, he reasoned, bargaining would be more productive. He designed and sold to both parties a five-day training program to improve the rapport between key company and union officials while at the same time maintaining their arm's-length relationship. Management was fearful and the union took a "What have we got to lose?" attitude. Both agreed to the meeting. The program went well. By the third day both parties were talking with candor about plant problems. It was, in fact, going too well. The union became suspicious. Old distrust of management set in. Union officials forgot the power of collaboration and felt something was being done to them—they didn't understand. The program ended when on the fourth night union members stormed out.

Brad lost the battle, but he is winning the war. He reported learning three things. First, both union and management have to spend time with their own people getting their acts together before they sit down to improve their bargaining relationships. Second, both must understand and agree to the training agenda ahead of time. Third, the union must be willing to share overhead costs.

The company labor climate has slowly and markedly improved over the years. Brad continues to bring people together to develop understanding of their mutual concerns. Because he keeps his word and eschews politics, he is widely trusted. By working to strengthen both sides, he is able to expand the areas of trust and cooperation between labor and management when they sit down across the bargaining table.

The Adult on its own tends toward monotony and "automaticity," while the Child on its own tends to become distracting. "Automaticity" refers to the machinelike quality of thinking. Alone, the Adult's functions are limited and repetitive. Adult thinking has a predictable quality. Some theorists, recognizing the limitations of thinking without Parent and Child, chide: "The mind is stupid."

The OK Child is often judged to be the most important ego state since it is not limited by rationality or by the historical determinations of the Parent. It brings depth, joy, and transcendence to life. Fortunate are those who can bring the OK Child to their social transactions. Increasing employee competence means creating conditions that enable employees to strengthen the three ego states individually and in relationship.

Tommy was the new-style plant manager of a Southern textile mill. He took over the job from a manager whose slogan was "I can run this plant because I'm the most intelligent person here." The old-style manager was proud of having risen through the ranks and claimed there was no job in the mill he couldn't do. He seemed intent on making employees feel less important than himself and appeared to tolerate having others work for him. Tommy, by contrast, had an attractive and secure Child. He easily admitted he didn't know all he needed to know.

Tommy understood that success was dependent on all workers doing their part. He soon knew all employees by their first names. There were 460 in the plant. Walking through the plant with him was a singular experience. People nodded, smiled, waved, and called out greetings. Tommy moved easily and acknowledged those he saw with a hello, handshake, slap on the back, or question about business problems. He discussed family developments and local athletic affairs familiarly. He definitely was a "good old boy."

Tommy expended no effort in putting on a magic show. When business issues were raised, he listened carefully, helped others define likely alternatives, and encouraged them to pursue the best one. Seldom have I seen a man so open to learning, to taking in new information. He soaked up knowledge like a blotter, Tommy's contribution to technical discussions was often formidable. Since he wasn't defensive and didn't have to win, subordinates readily came to him with requests or ideas. When a subordinate's idea challenged him, he was delighted. When he saw the wheel being reinvented, he set the petitioner straight with gentle humor.

Two other things astonished me about Tommy. His values did not intrude into business discussions, yet he was crystal-clear about right and wrong. Under his predecessor, corruption had been accepted as a cost of doing business. Everyone had a price. Two ex-managers were under indictment for fraudulent billing practices. Management had grown lax about keeping the plant effluents clean so as not to pollute local water sources. In addition, purchasing practices tended to favor certain suppliers without regard to competitive bidding. When these matters surfaced, Tommy astonished us all. With vigor, he rejected shoddy practices. He simply understood that good business was based on integrity and would tolerate no less. There was no condemnation. He refused to believe his subordinates had ever acted in any other way.

It is hard to remove corrupt practices once they have been established as "normal" in the system. Anyone who seeks to change them is seen as a Pollyanna, unrealistic, not understanding about these things. Employees are swept up in the net and soon accept such practices as standard operating procedure. When they benefit from them, they hesitate to change them. They'd rather not face their complicity. Tommy handled it exactly right. He simply assumed everyone was honest. Few wanted to fail him in his generous assumption.

Another startling and refreshing thing about Tommy was that he told his superiors the truth. If an unpopular person or cause was right, it received support from Tommy. If a peer was equivocating at a senior staff meeting, he questioned the presenter carefully until he or she came clean. Tommy's behavior was neither strategy nor device. That's just the way he was. He was totally clear about the need for openness and trust in creating a powerful company able to survive in the face of complex production and marketing problems. His high intelligence and natural affection for others made him a highly successful motivator of workers. Tommy helped make people more "intelligent"—that is, he helped them liberate their Adult and empower their Child.

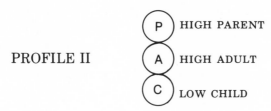

PROFILE II

P   HIGH PARENT

A   HIGH ADULT

C   LOW CHILD

The Parent ego state gets its power from the peculiarities of the childhood conditioning process. The rules of life are bestowed by parents with a special force and coloring. Since such rules always cover important topics like sex, politics, religion, nationalism, and race, parents consider it vitally important to get the message across. Sibling rejection of familial values reflects negatively on parents. Thus they feel justified in enforcing their position strenuously. This conditioning occurs at a time when parents are the sole source of life's banes and blessings. Obedience and rebellion are very purple words. They get this heavy load from early childhood experiences with praise and blame. It is standard for parents to withhold affection when their rules are transgressed and to bestow love when they are obeyed. Given infant dependency, it is hard to imagine a more irresistible process. When parents are determined to instill their own beliefs and behavior in their offspring, the outcome, except in exceptional circumstances, is predetermined.

Part of this early parenting usually includes warnings against deviance from "the tried and true," "the way of our fathers," and "the one true faith." Shame, that most painful human experience, is revived by going against what we believe to be true. A large proportion of worker behavior arises out of this source—parental tapes replaying in their heads. Because of its repetitive and "closed" quality, this phenomenon is referred to as "positionality." When these circuits are operative, people are not responsive to new insights. They go around on "automatic."

High Parent employees are not aware of how artificial and rigid their behavior is. This explains why they exhibit the same behavior over and over no matter how distasteful the results. It's as if they were being controlled by an old computer program in their heads.

The concept of script explains this high degree of behavioral predictability. Each person early in life works out a preset drama along with a cast of characters, acts, roles, and dialogues. The whole thing is based on the dynamics of infancy. Thus we relate to certain people and are forever barred from those who do not fit our act. Some scripts are for losers. Winner scripts summon the best from the individual, assume the most positive social arrangements, and lead to success and happiness.

We use manipulative roles to attract others to our magic show. Most everyone has played these inauthentic roles. Stephen Karpman designates them as persecutor, victim, and rescuer.* Those in positions of power who impose unreasonable or unfair demands on others, particularly when others have little hope of defending themselves, are rightly called persecutors.

Victims too can be manipulative. We have all known those who whine and complain their way through the day about problems they will never face. They are often excellent actors. Shoulders hunched, hands trembling, voice showing the right amount of concern, they pass the time seeking out persecutors or rescuers on whom to run their rap.

---

* Stephen Karpman, "Script Drama Analysis," *Transactional Analysis Bulletin,* Vol. 7, No. 26 (1968), pp. 39–43.

Rescuers, too, are "doing their thing." They make themselves feel good by putting others in their debt. Who, after all, would not be grateful for help? Rescuers are full of answers to questions nobody is asking. They inflict advice or assistance on others. It is called "helping the hell out of someone." Rescuers put people under their control and build dependency. It is easy to make yourself feel good by proffering what you see as help. It is difficult for others to resist what seems to be offered in good will. The rule is: Help is beneficial only if it seems like help to others. It is difficult to give helpful help.

High Parent, High Adult, Low Child managers may be masters of the manipulative roles described above. They are mobilized by old-style injunctions, internalized from domineering and moralistic parents:

Never trust anyone.
Winning isn't everything; it's the only thing.
Do it well or don't do it.
Cream always rises to the top.
Wasting time is wasting money.
If you can't stand the heat . . . .
There are two kinds of people: winners and losers.
There's one born every minute.
Life is a jungle where only the fit survive.

The list is endless. To managers caught in this headlock, every day provides evidence to support their cynicism. They are trapped in self-fulfilling prophecy. They are most comfortable being with those of their own stripe. They experience high levels of discomfort when alone. The company is a place for continual diversion.

Work is everything for such managers. Their active intelligence gives power to their parental scripting. When not engaged in work, they withdraw for rest and relaxation, only to plan their next move. They consider pastimes wasteful and avoid ritual unless it furthers their game plan. With little available Child, they are strangers to intimacy. For them, intimacy is an interesting diversion from the important business of work.

The president and administrator of one company I worked with was known as the "Green Machine." Green was an exciting and challenging man. Continually seeking new worlds to conquer, he was intolerant of those who could not share his visions or maintain his pace. He did not see his own shortcomings with the same clarity that he saw others'. Lacking a softer side, he was sometimes ruthless in firing people. Three kinds of people survived in his company: those who had some trait he admired, those he felt were "appreciative," and those he could coerce or direct.

Subordinates dealt with him cagily. Adult-Adult transactions could quickly turn into attacks with one misstep. Parent-Child was his dominant style. He made decisions and expected them to be carried out. He discussed plans with others only to get their ideas or to evaluate the risks he faced. His decision making contributed nothing to motivation. Communication was all downward. The company climate was tense and gamey, and rumors abounded. Extensive effort was spent "covering your ass."

Secrecy, even about little things, was considered important. There were A-B-C distribution lists for internal company correspondence. No one was quite sure how he or she got on a list. Managers met clandestinely at airports and other places to find out what was going on in the company. The extensive effort put into maintaining company "secrets" was based on Green's assumptions that only some employees could be trusted. In general, he saw others as lazy, selfish, untrustworthy, and in need of constant supervision. "Span of control" and industrial engineering were his big interests. Since fear was his mode of control, people accepted goals overtly, but there was a high degree of internal resistance.

The company prospered under Green. It had a significant

piece of the market. The financial people were bright and knew how to run money. Green assumed all the risks and made all the decisions. Others were willing to let him do so. It made their job a lot simpler. Most important, under Green's firm hand, they could move quickly and effectively in making acquisitions. His motto was "No guts, no glory." When Green made a misstep, which he seldom did, it was memorable. In the middle of a complicated, unfriendly takeover attempt, he died. Green's company is slowly adjusting to a more open and collaborative style.

PROFILE III

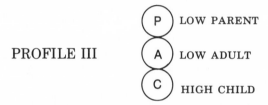

P) LOW PARENT

A) LOW ADULT

C) HIGH CHILD

The Child ego state has energy, creativity, spontaneity, and authenticity—all the things that make an individual attractive. It is the source of intuition and the route to the unconscious. In the Child are those dimensions that make people "marvelous." People whose behavior is guided by their feelings are a constant source of wonder. They clearly march to other music. Their tunes, even when strange, may be compelling. Child-dominant managers have a way of reasoning all their own. They figure things out their way and get to people easily. Generally, they do not have a well-defined Parent; their Child's standards guide them. Zany, zestful, flamboyant, they are willing to try the new. Often they are found in sales and marketing or training and development. Sometimes they are attracted to creative industries like advertising and media production.

It was said repeatedly of Mike that he was the most important man in the company. "The company could not run without him" was a common remark. He headed sales. People were naturally drawn to him, even though his behavior was unusual. Mike's idea of a sales meeting was calling the national sales force to a West Coast city to see if they could drink it dry in three days. Child-dominant himself, he could see only the Child in others. Golf, shows, and the best restaurants in town were his style. There were few substantive issues on his agenda. Problems between friends had a way of working out. Lectures on motivation and contemporary sales techniques were interludes in the festivities. Mike expected his people to be there but not to take it seriously.

Mike did not know how to talk straight about important or difficult subjects. You had to listen carefully to his jokes, because he was often trying to tell you something. You knew something was up if Mike asked you to dinner. You'd start drinking around seven, eat around ten, and sometime after midnight, thoroughly drunk, Mike would indirectly tell you what he had on his mind. Two salesmen I knew were fired on such occasions and rehired the next morning. Mike often found it necessary to sleep at the "wayside hotel"—his euphemism for a gas station. He'd go home with the sunrise, shower and shave, and be ready to work at 9:00 A.M.

Mike had a warm and friendly manner. He liked people readily and wanted things to go well. His humor was often gently barbed. Equals would have dismissed him on a number of grounds, but they couldn't deny his successful sales figures. Much of his drinking and late hours had a desperate quality. It seemed ironic that he prospered in a self-destructive way. He hardly ever gave clear orders to subordinates. They seldom knew where they stood with him.

I once asked Mike why he was so successful. His reply went like this:

I really don't know. People seem to like to do business with me. I don't know why they do it, but a customer will order a tank car of acid and I'll send him one of base. The next day he'll call me and complain because I didn't send him acid. "I'll keep the base," he'll say to me, "and will you please expedite the acid today?" I don't know why they do it.

As salesmen, Child-dominant managers add charm and energy to an often trying role and make the tedious seem easy and natural. All of us have this power within us—the spellbinding charm of the Natural Child. Unfortunately, many of us simply haven't learned to use it. It is our recognition of this potential in us that makes Child-dominant people so attractive. They hook the bright, cheerful, and fun-loving in us. We like ourselves better by being around those who make the Child work for us.

High Child, Low Parent, Low Adult managers are not big on rote learning or walking in others' footsteps. They find the resource of their own Child rich and rewarding. They like the friends, energy, and fun they create. They often enjoy fashioning unusual solutions to problems or doing what others said can't be done. Often they are unable or unwilling to adjust to the demands of the organization and may not stay in one place too long. Some companies, aware that such people are a valuable resource, make adjustments to accommodate them, cherishing their own "crazy" types. "They protect me like the Soldiers and Sailors monument," says one manager of a *Fortune* 500 company who wears an eye patch and talks a lot about love. "One man with a beard in this company is enough," the president of another company said to a bearded development officer who had saved the company millions.

Child-dominant types may be so attractive that they become victims of their own success. As idealists, they can be diverted from the central task of the company. They are often thought to be more concerned with people than production. Sometimes they can be lured away from the straight and narrow by the siren call of shortcuts to easy profits or the hope of "making a killing." "Nobody," they rationalize, "is watching. I'm so unimportant they'll overlook me." In this they show the weakness of not having a sound Parent and Adult. They function best with firm but gentle control.

Working with professionals who have only their distracted Child available can be a frustrating experience. Frank was company counsel. He was an authority on tax law and knew his numbers. If you let him control the conversation, he would drive you crazy. He jumped from one topic to another, never finishing anything. I've had several discussions with him and often had the feeling we'd never get out of the thicket. Frank won't answer questions directly. Sometimes he doesn't even hear them. He hears a buzzword and just begins talking. He won't respond to a question in a way the petitioner can deal with. Talking with him, I often find myself agreeing to things I don't understand. I rationalize, "He must know what he's talking about even if I don't. And I don't want to look dumb."

Besides being easily distracted by the phone, someone passing the office, or a new idea streaking across his mind, Frank fatigues easily. If the subject is complex, he will stay with it only up to a point; then he will weary and search for an easy way out: "I have some other matters to attend to now— let's continue this tomorrow." "I'll discuss this further with George before I decide what we should do." "I guess we've gone about as far as we can go on this."

Dominated by his distracted Child, Frank has no tolerance for conflict. His theme is "Getting by, by going along." He considers disagreements to be in bad taste and to demonstrate a weakness of character. He does not enjoy the robust pleasures of matching wits, struggling for position, searching for clarity, or challenging someone else. Struggle is not his thing. He defines himself according to what he thinks and likes, thereby avoiding tension or stress. He relishes his good-guy act.

I have worked out a tactic called "muscling the process" for dealing with the Franks of this world. First, I am candid about my needs and the reasons for our meeting. I admit that I do not want a random conversation and am unwilling to waste time. I request a contract to let me control the process so I can expeditiously get my own needs met.

"Muscling the process" is a way of getting a lot of information across in a short period of time. It works like this:

1. I interrupt the respondent's line of thought when I understand where he or she is going. The phrase "I've got it, go on" stops lengthy discussions on points that are clear and pushes the speaker to the next item.
2. I stop excursiveness. "I don't need to know any more on that subject" stops the speaker from going off on tangents and refocuses him or her on what I need to know.
3. I ask questions for definition. "Please define 'float' for me." Questioning the respondent is a quick way to get inside his or her thought processes.

By muscling the process, I have been able to work successfully with those who have insufficient control over their own thinking. When respondents adamantly insist that I don't understand what they're going to say, of course I hear them out fully.

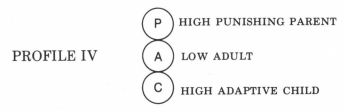

PROFILE IV

P) HIGH PUNISHING PARENT

A) LOW ADULT

C) HIGH ADAPTIVE CHILD

Here is a common profile: managers whose behavior, unmediated by the Adult, swings between two dramatic ego states. One moment warm and friendly, they show a desire to be liked. They are mannerly, concerned, and friendly. Often, when surprised or under stress, they quickly shift to the Parent and become judgmental, punitive, and domineering. Their behavior has a love-hate quality. After subordinates have been caught off guard a couple of times by the shift from Child to Parent, they tend to become defensive and suspicious. As noted earlier, our scripting controls our behavior quite apart from whatever is going on about us. Discovery of the Parent ego state clarifies how artificial much script behavior really is. If you ask people a question when their Parent is turned on, they will give you a preprogrammed answer. As the discussion proceeds, they will restate their position again and again, much like a broken record. Then you realize that's all there is to it. They've run their rap, done their thing. Not open to new ideas, they're reduced to playing their tune over and over.

Parent-dominant people are limited in their thinking. Questions of substance may be met with evasive responses like these: "We've survived for 10 years; we must be doing something right." "If other people know more about this than we do, I don't know who they are." Another evasive response is the ad hominem argument: "If you're so smart, how come you're not rich?" All these responses close off the topic, as any Adult present will see. If Parent types are unwilling to acknowledge their limitations, transactions with them will not go far. Ironically, because they are assertive and state their position with conviction, to the uninitiated they appear to be "competent" and "leaders."

Another clue to Parent-dominant managers is their inability to ask and answer questions directly. They will go off on tangents, sometimes at length. They will answer a question with another question or use leading questions—those that have built-in answers to make their point or set someone up. They may ask two questions in a row, not waiting for an answer, or give an answer that is contradicted by their behavior. They will fight questions on the grounds of irrelevancy or inappropriateness. Communicating with such people is hard work. They are manipulating to maintain their own position.

Scripts are complex operations. To free ourselves from them, we need to analyze our ego states, characteristic transactions, games, and time structuring. Analysis of household dramas of youth, life positions, and injunctions are further tools. Tabi Kahler and Hedges Capers have pointed out that people can act out their whole scripted lives in one transaction.* These instant dramas are called miniscripts. Under the influence of drivers like "Be perfect" or "Be strong," people with a strong Parent act out in minutes their whole "magic show"—their act. Three other internal injunctions—"Try hard," "Please me," and "Hurry up"—keep these people from managing their lives. These drivers help them maintain their Not OK position in life and power their manipulative roles.

The other half of this profile is the High Adaptive Child (AC), which propels these managers to seek self-approval and group acceptance. If they have come through the ranks, they are AC competent. They can cite statistics on yesterday's game for whatever sport is in season. They read *The New York Times* and *The Wall Street Journal* regularly. Their political and religious thought never moves far from center. They know the best restaurants. Unobtrusively, they report their credentials and whose confidence they share. They dress well and carry themselves easily. When you know about their travels, they do not bore you with details. Their magic show is no small accomplishment. Many have tried and failed to pull it off. When it is done well, it appears effortless. It is, however, completely adaptive—an exquisite adjustment to the environment. All of us have a magic show, but not all of us believe in it so wholeheartedly that we forget it's only an act.

High Parent, Low Adult, High Adaptive Child managers are underpowered in the control tower. Many problems cannot be solved either by friendliness or conviction. They lack the hard focus of High Adult people who use the best available technol-

* Tabi Kahler and Hedges Capers, "The Miniscript," *Transactional Analysis Journal,* January 1974.

ogy and are able to take appropriate risks. When their Child is dominant, they tend to put off a problem until it is inescapable. Then, instead of cathecting their Adult and solving the problem, they shift to the Parent and charge. They can be heard worrying: "If people would only do what they're supposed to." Or "How am I going to run this place with the people personnel sends me?" In the face of problems they can't charm away, they attack, frequently making a bad situation worse. Their win-lose, love-hate behavior is vexing. This type of manager is the "double-minded man, unstable in all his ways" of whom the Bible spoke (James 1:8).

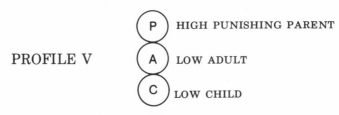

PROFILE V

P   HIGH PUNISHING PARENT

A   LOW ADULT

C   LOW CHILD

One employee said of her boss, "He learned management from Hitler." Events in the life of this type of manager have a memorable quality. Friends and nonfriends find themselves years later retelling vignettes of their employment. With excluded Child and weakened Adult not always available for reality testing, such managers are left under control of the angry Parent. They can be dangerous.

Jack was financial officer and member of the company's bargaining team. Known for his ability to lose his temper, he had struck subordinates on at least two occasions and kicked down a door on another. Not the company spokesman, he had sat silently through many hours of acrimonious bargaining. Two weeks after the contract expired, feeling bargaining was getting nowhere, the union decided to set up a picket line. They notified reporters of their intention.

On the first day of the strike, as management crossed the line, there were shouts and heckling. When Jack appeared, pickets jeered. Predictably, Jack got out of his car, walked over to the nearest picketer, and slugged him. A press photographer recorded the event. The picture appeared that evening in the city newspaper under the caption "Here's how labor relations are practiced at National Widget." When Jack recalls the event, he reports: "The next thing I knew I was on the bottom of a howling, screaming mob. I said to myself, Jack, what are you doing here? You don't belong here." The incident had expensive consequences for the company. Jack spent 30 days in jail.

Boisterous in temperament, macho in style, this type of manager is convinced that people cannot be trusted, winning is all that counts, and "if you don't take them first, they'll take you." Such managers enjoy telling war stories—how others got wasted, smashed, or pulverized. Their language is rich with metaphors of battle, never letting down, win-lose, and surviving against the odds. Strike first is their wisdom. Keep 'em off balance. When others laugh, they cackle. They have difficulty telling their friends from their enemies.

Thrasher was an officer with a difference. Whatever he did he did big. Other people took vacations; he played golf at Hilton Head with Arnie Palmer. Other people drove cars; he traded in his Cadillac Eldorado every year. Some had a good dinner companion; he ate with the French ambassador. Most of his friends lived in houses; he rattled around in 15 rooms. Others were educated; he had a licentiate in particle physics from the Sorbonne. Shaking hands with him was always an arm wrestle. His voice was loud.

Thrasher could be gently demeaning when talking to someone he clearly thought was dull normal. He would ask leading questions, leaving the impression that anyone who disagreed wasn't too bright. He had an interesting attack style. He would explode unexpectedly and catch workers off guard. Then he would quickly deflate and talk in a normal voice, leaving an "edge" in the room. He would attack others for a goof or a bungle. When under attack himself, he would feel humiliated and distressed. There were no norms in the company encouraging others to defend the person under attack or limit the aggressor. Thrasher was quite alone. Everyone worked at pleasing Thrasher no matter what the consequences. On substantive matters, he could be very weak.

A high point was reached one day during an executive meeting session. The committee was examining a comparative cost study on a number of computer main frames. Thrasher took the position that the report was superfluous and everyone should simply listen to him. His experience made him the smartest person in the room. Much time and haggling could be saved if others simply agreed with his recommendation. Astonished by this assertion of superiority, a salesman in the room repeatedly brought the discussion back to technical matters, supporting his own cost-benefit analysis. Driven too far by reason, Thrasher leaped to his feet, flung open his jacket, and pointed to the label, shouting: "See that? Yves St. Laurent. You guys will never afford the clothes I wear." The chairman called a hasty coffee break to restore decorum.

In an old-style organization people like Thrasher often "win" because no one will take them on. Ordinary people don't want to go that crazy. Such managers can often be found in higher echelons where aggressiveness is mistaken for competence, assertiveness for confidence, and bellicosity for leadership. When the pressure mounts, these managers lose effective Adult control. Behavior then is not based in reality. The disconsolate Child retreats and turns control over to the Parent. This explains a curious phenomenon: Some Parent types attack without being angry at their victims. After the dust-up, they expect things to get quickly back to normal and may seem surprised when the victim looks hurt and angry. "Nothing personal, you understand," they mutter. Angry display is simply the way they do it. By causing employees pain and stimulating rebellion in the organization, they often make the problem worse.

Our best resource in problem solving is the Adult—in particular, the collective Adult resources of the team. When managers are unable to mobilize these resources in themselves and others, the likelihood of failure increases dramatically.

High Parent, Low Adult, Low Child managers often view life through a conspiratorial lens. It makes their crazy behavior more tolerable. They believe that somewhere, someplace, someone is in charge of this mess. Somebody understands. Somebody has the necessary power. Somebody is responsible. They seek to deny the destructive consequences of their behavior on the grounds that since no one takes care of them, they don't have to take responsibility for others. They may carry their conspiratorial thesis to absurd lengths to avoid taking responsibility. Their rationalizations—and they are numerous—are all of the "life is a jungle" variety. They believe they have mountains of evidence daily to support their cynicism. I have watched these destructive types grow in status and power on their manipulative ability as persecutors. They create a house of cards to maintain their particular craziness.

Charlie was chief operating officer of a Southwestern company in the energy business. He reported directly to the president and chief executive officer. The first thing always said about Charlie was that he graduated at the head of his class at business school. This seemed to validate anything he did, no matter how destructive. "Anyone that smart," people reasoned, "must know what he's doing." Without the reality-based Adult or hooking behavior of the Child, he was left solely with his Punishing Parent. Truth is stranger than fiction. Events around Charlie continually had a high dramatic quality. At any moment he could "fly off the handle" with threats, shouts, and personal abuse. Heavy politics, secrecy, and cynical conversation were constants in his life. Subordinates always reacted to Charlie with amazement. "How does he get away with it? How come the president lets this go on? There oughta be a law."

Charlie hired a labor negotiator away from a competitor by offering him a significant salary increase. He fired the man 14 days later, astonished because the new hand told the truth. This simply was not part of labor relations as Charlie understood them. Two subordinates were in the slammer for 90 days for alleged kickbacks. They pleaded no contest. A unit manager reported, "When I came to work a year ago, I was a reasonable man. Today I'm a screaming maniac. Do you think," he asked poignantly, "it means anything that I fainted at dinner last night?"

Charlie found a consultant who "understood" him. He would hire or promote no one without his guru's approval. Said a psychologist to a new employee: "If you can stand Charlie for six months, you've got it made." Surreptitiously questioning subordinates and secretaries and examining the contents of their wastebaskets was part of his style. The only manager to survive Charlie was one who could swear effectively. He would unload on Charlie in private. Anyone, Charlie figured, who behaved that badly could be his friend. At exit interviews, departing managers uniformly described Charlie as a tyrant.

Why did Charlie get away with it? There are several reasons. Others in the company bought into the rap "that business is a jungle where only the fit survive." They erroneously assumed destructive behavior was normal in successful companies. "Don't all companies run this way?" "Isn't this how people should behave?" Others in the company simply accepted what was given. They lacked the training in process and behavior management to resist the depredations of destructive managers.

Charlie cannot be approached about the long-term benefits of good employee morale. He continues to hire new people and burn them out. He will be gone in a few years and it will be somebody else's problem. Irresponsibly unconcerned about others, indifferent to what employees do to each other, lacking vision and integrity, he struggles to stay on top by staying ahead. The long-term health of the company is someone else's worry. If he makes his, who cares?

Managers who are dominated by the angry Parent are vulnerable on four counts:

1. Despite their bluster and braggadocio, they exercise far less control over their units than the casual observer may think. Their behavior works against them, generating resistance and rebellion. They need others to play the Adaptive Child to their Punishing Parent so they can maintain their Not OK position. Subordinates need the boss's excesses to maintain their "If It Weren't For Them" games. Soon the whole organization is enrolled in games and politics. Such an organization can be highly symbiotic—everyone needs everyone else's craziness.

Many years ago as a young professional, I discovered how curiously integrated many old-style power-on systems really are. I was asked by a division president to work with the head of one of his distribution centers. The president reported he had no influence over Ted. Whenever he asked him to do something, Ted nodded agreeably, made notes to himself on 3" × 5" cards, and did nothing. In this old, family-owned company, obedience to superiors was assumed to have little influence on business success in a highly competitive sector of the petrochemical field. Sometimes Ted was merely noncommittal about the president's wishes. But noncommittal or agreeable, he simply didn't do what the president requested. This seemed strange to me because the senior officer was a reasonable, clear-headed, and patient man.

As I examined Ted's organization closely, I found relatively high levels of resistance among all 45 employees at the distribution center. The president had asked me to look at the center because of excessive grievances.

One day when the president's cabinet met, it was clear from watching Ted that he was either not listening or indifferent to what was being said. The discussions simply did not interest him. He was busy with his own internal agenda. I confronted him on his behavior. "Ted," I said, "I have worked with you for six months. It is clear to me you don't listen to the president. Or, if you listen, you don't care to follow his leadership. You have not in the past done what he tells you. You are not doing it now. And you don't intend to do it in the future." Ted seemed totally calm about my confrontation. A sheepish grin spread across his face as he admitted this was so. It was one of those moments of truth. Everyone there understood. Six months later Ted took early retirement.

Companies that place great value on obedience either generate high rebellion or adapt by hiring only High Parent and Adaptive Child types. Such companies can function reasonably well if they are not faced with need to cope with rapid change and shifting market conditions.

2. Heavy Parent types are relatively easy to manipulate. If you push their button, they go out of control. They become unconscious and go into their act. It doesn't take subordinates long to find out where the Parent manager's buttons are. Any time they wish to direct attention away from themselves or from real problems, they simply push the button and set the boss off. Victims and persecutors often have an equal power over each other. Driving persecutors crazy, diminishing their options, causing them to overreact, and preying on their suspicions are age-old tactics of the oppressed. It is the absence of the intervening Adult that makes High Parent types vulnerable.

3. Since they are closed to new data and feel comfortable only with the familiar, Parent-dominant managers are vulnerable to changes in market conditions, technological breakthroughs, new cost-cutting strategies, and the like. They are totally taken up with the status quo. They simply do not have the mechanism to cope with oncoming change. They will find themselves outdistanced by competitors with a fresh approach and a more open and flexible style.

4. Because Parent-dominant types tend to limit their contacts to a few of their own feather, they are vulnerable to all the emotional and physical ills of social isolates. They are not strengthened by the give-and-take of meeting everyday challenges. Often there is an accompanying emotional arteriosclerosis.

PROFILE VI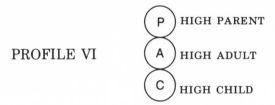

People who have all three ego states fully developed and available for appropriate use are the most attractive and competent employees. Their consciousness is a powerful blend of the three operational ego states. Used singly, each state is fully competent. Used dynamically, the three synergize, creating immense potency.

These people often seem bigger than life. Everything seems to work for them. I use the term "synamic" (a combination of "dynamic" and "synergistic") to describe them. When faced with complex problems, they function quietly yet intently, gathering all available data on the topic. Deploying their staff to collect, organize, and analyze data, they search out new alternatives and develop option lists with cost-benefit analyses. Aware of the shortcomings of intellectualizing, they will listen carefully to intuitive analysis and encourage subordinates to argue their best hunches in the matter. They are sensitive to the time when action is called for and make necessary decisions with ease.

Aware that decision making is only the first step in the process, they develop support plans, midcourse correction points, and evaluative criteria with subordinates. Basic to their success is the ability to achieve 100 percent effort from their subordinates and to distribute ownership of company goals. Their ability to deploy human resources has high motivational payoff. They demonstrate caring easily toward all employees, not as a function of their job or to promote their status, but as an expression of themselves. It is simply who they are. It is powerful modeling for all employees.

Ron heads a medium-size plant in the Midwest. It is a pleasure walking beside him through the plant. Employees at all levels are comfortable with him and express pleasure at seeing him. He seems to have a prodigious memory. He seldom fails to remember spouses' and children's names and important recent events in people's lives. It is clear that employees return his caring. He has legitimated support behavior for everyone.

In the taxonomy of feelings, caring is often listed among those considered "soft." Related to this is the concern of some managers that an organization based on reason and nurturance will become indolent and unable to face the rigors of competition. These managers fear that pleasant feelings will displace "true grit" and weaken the employee's will to do what's necessary. Feelings will confuse the Adult's ability to see things as they are. They will turn the brain to silly-putty. Feelings are fleeting and make people vulnerable, so why bother? Of what value is "growth" if it means people will do only a little more of what they are already doing? "If caring makes you weak in the knees, more of the same may melt the spine." All these misconceptions clear up with experience. The world really does work. Most fears of this kind turn out to be groundless.

In fact, more of everything operates in the person with three fully functioning ego states. The Adult overrides the Child's fears and, should matters turn grave, summons help from the Parent to do what needs to be done. I asked a manager recently if development made her feel weak. "No," she replied, "I never felt stronger." When matters are grave, we can't afford to risk the future on those who aren't functioning on all three cylinders. We will always need all the fully functioning people we can find.

Another vital characteristic of synamic managers is that they are incorruptible. They do not hold honesty as a position. They don't consider whether at this time it would be beneficial to lie, steal, or corrupt others. They don't have to think about being honest. With all ego states functioning in an integrated way, they just are honest. There is no other alternative. Any of the three ego states, from its independent perspective, can provide reasons for denying the value of openness and candor. But all three, operating together, prevent fully functioning managers from sacrificing their integrity.

The opposite of honesty is not dishonesty. The opposite of the truth is not a lie. The issue is more complex. It is difficult in many situations to know what's so. Key data is often missing, human biases present, future options uncertain, competitors' challenges unclear, and operation principles ambiguous. When the situation is fluid, the subtleties of both knowing and reporting the truth are exposed. Many managers, of course, deny these complexities by referring the problem to the Parent and solving it in traditional ways. They are literalists who see things simply and respond certainly in the way they always have.

The task is not so easy for new-style managers. They have a great many variables to factor into their decision making. They need to pull together all available data, finely tune decisions about others' maturity, and sharpen their intuitive skills. Telling the truth can be an exceedingly subtle process. New-style managers are tentative, always open, awaiting new data and fresh insights.

The power of fully functioning managers lies in their firm hold on reality. They see the world as it is. They factor values and feelings into their thinking. They cannot be led far astray for very long. They have a self-correcting mechanism. They win and lose like everyone else and invest no energy in continuing on self-defeating paths. They refuse to send good emotional energy after bad.

Easygoing, comfortable with himself, free to care for others, always a good student, Wolfe was head of production in a major pharmaceuticals firm. His easy affections made him a favorite of the whole division. Professional, technical, and operational employees all spoke highly of him. They were proud to be in his division and looked for opportunities to serve him better. His division continually beat carefully set production goals and was always open to new ideas and techniques. Production introduced a number of innovations that were useful throughout the company.

Top executives admired their production head, despite the continual challenges he brought to them. Wolfe had no internal resistance to "telling it like it is." He simply spoke the truth and easily expressed his feelings. He showed anger and mild scorn at overdeliberate peers who enjoyed executive games and perquisites more than problem solving. Team membership was never easy for him. Yet he and his division set the pace for energy, profits, good sense, and hard work.

When Wolfe began riding a motorcycle to work and strode through the plant with a jumpsuit covering his casual clothes, executive eyebrows were raised. He dismissed questions about his personal habits as irrelevant. His sense of self worked against him among those who valued conformity. Because he stood out so much, other companies hesitated to consider him for a position. They were unwilling to accept the challenge of his strength. This despite a spectacular record. He received many promotions and prospered in his own company.

Synamic managers are most attractive and competent. "Charismatic," "natural," and "proven" are words often used to describe them. They are dynamic and growth-oriented. They don't need others to be complete. They are often high-energy people who survive on five hours sleep a night. They radiate aliveness. They take care of themselves, ensuring that they receive life-giving strokes to their Parent, Adult, and Child. They can ask for help and function well in teams. They are self-actualizing people.

Their Adult is strong and easily available. When contamination appears, they recognize and accept responsibility for it. Committed to their own growth, they never expect to stop learning. They think clearly but are also aware of the limitations of cognition. Their Child ego state is open, warm, delightful, and easily available. It can readily be seen in the easy and free movement of their limbs. Their clear-headed rejection of politics and banality seems to the casual viewer to be unfriendly. And in the short term it is. They respond easily and patiently to those whose friendship they value. They may restimulate Not OK in lesser folk. They attract the best in growth-oriented workers. They appear to be people of a higher order. Indeed, they may be the ultimate social creatures—the leaders of the future who enable others to achieve higher social consciousness.

PROFILE VII

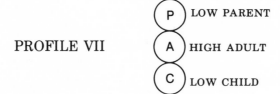

P) LOW PARENT

A) HIGH ADULT

C) LOW CHILD

Adult-dominant managers face work with only their thinking operative. Their feelings are so highly adaptive that these managers are often unable to form meaningful relationships. Their social structuring lacks firmness and substance. Found sometimes in the ranks of engineers, scientists, and accountants, they are often fact, number, and object oriented. They are effective in short-term problems, but because they lack explicit values and Child energy, they may not fare well over the long haul.

Jim is an engineer with an automotive company. He took the

PAC Self-Scoring Profile and scored low on the Parent side. Since this is unusual, I questioned him about it. He reported that he was born in China of English parents and at the age of four moved to Singapore, where he was raised until adolescence. He graduated from high school in the United States during World War II and served in the infantry. Captured by the Germans, he spent three brutal years in a prisoner-of-war camp. He admitted he didn't know who he was. "The saddest thing in my life," he said, "was telling my son he would have to find out who he was on his own because I couldn't help him." The sense of definition that comes from understanding one's roots and development was missing in Jim. He couldn't identify his background, be proud of it, or make sense of it. So he excluded it.

On rare occasions when he was drunk, Jim would report on life as a prisoner of war and the men he had killed. Much emotional material in Jim's life remained undigested. He coped with this unmediated load by excluding it. It was just too painful and confusing to handle. Having excluded both Parent and Child, Jim was left with only his Adult to manage his life.

Within these severe limitations he did very well. As an engineer, he found a niche with others who shared his knowledge. Relations with Jim tended to be friendly and lacked depth. Jim found it impossible to take a stand on his own. He waited patiently for the boss to establish a position; then Jim carried it out wholeheartedly. Other engineers sometimes saw Jim as a "cipher." Indeed, he often took the position of the last person he talked to.

Jim was a "survivor" and was politically oriented. He lacked candor and the willingness to see problems clearly. His early life experiences made him doubt the trustworthiness of others. This cynicism created unnecessary communications difficulties for his division and strained vendor relations—a problem that proved costly on a couple of occasions. A difficult man to work with, Jim coped admirably considering his foreshortened personality.

The pathway is difficult for those who choose to function without feelings and social structuring. People with this profile are reminiscent of computers or robots. Their major difficulty is working with others. Their behavior is often repetitious and boring, their relationships sterile and unfeeling.

7

The Parent Ego State

When we say there are three distinct ego states that arise out of different sources, have different consequences, and are experienced differently, we mean that you can choose which one you will use. You can shift your consciousness into the ego state most suitable to the moment. You can choose how you will act or react, what you will feel, and what prejudices you will hold.

This chapter shows you the options available to you by demonstrating how the mind works. When you see how it works you will do the right thing—that's part of human elegance. Not to be aware of your options increases the likelihood of failure, or of making a less than optimal choice. Indeed, this appears a too likely possibility. Learning how your mind works and developing the skills to use it is a fundamental part of any development program. It maximizes social potential.

In general, experience teaches us that workers use too much Parent, too little OK Child, and not enough Adult, as shown in the left column below. The profile, achieved after training, is shown on the right.

	Before Training	*After Training*
P	70%	20%
A	20%	40%
C	10%	40%

Whatever you do, if you are aware of and consider all three ego states and decide what results you wish, you can anticipate good results. One of the important changes to be sought is reduction of the Parent. This chapter will explain why.

THE SOURCE OF RESISTANCE

The Parent ego state is so familiar it is hard to see. Being so much a part of the social landscape, it becomes indistinguishable from the more conscious states of Child and Adult. It is the trees for the forest part of the metaphor. We enjoy great internal affirmation when we function in the Parent. Anything that feels so right must be the way to proceed. A closer look at the Parent ego state, particularly in times of transition or challenge, reveals serious problems. As significant and useful as the Parent is, it is also the source of much restrictive, controlling, punishing, and Not OK behavior. What Claude Steiner first called (now with some regret) the "Pig Parent" is the source of much of the world's troubles. There are five things structurally and functionally to report about this ego state.

1. The Parent contains all those things we absolutely believe to be true and stake our lives upon. We accept the content as given and irrevocable. We build the fabric of our social lives upon it. It encompasses our belief system, our sense of right and wrong. This ranges all the way from the proper sort of food to eat and clothes to wear through how to treat animals and prepare for a friend's visit. It includes our position on which political party or religion is the most reliable. It includes lists of what to condone, whom to respect, and what is permissible. It is the largest part of our personality and the most frequently expressed behavior. The average manager probably spends 70 percent of his or her time in the Parent. Twenty percent would be ideal.

2. Most Parent material is held without thinking. It is often

based on unexamined assumptions and is unsupported by fact. When we are in our Parent, we believe what we do is right without thinking about it. A secretary reported that as a child she shared with her father her concerns about faith and life. How, she queried, was Jonah able to survive in the whale? What did Jesus do to catch so many fish? How can I believe in an invisible God? "Believe, only believe," her father replied. Unsatisfactory in content, the Parent encourages a nonthinking, nonevidentiary approach to life.

The secretary's father scripted his young daughter with the indirect command "Don't think." As a result, she was left to face life scripted with his parental recordings and only her little-girl feelings of fear. She successfully pursued a nonthinking course through 40 years, accepting little else for herself than life as a secretary. With her Adult unavailable, she continually frustrated her self-interests. She unnecessarily limited herself and saw others as the cause of her behavior.

When the Parent is energized, thinking stops. We become unconscious and are not in touch with the here and now. Behavior is always the giveaway. When the Parent is mobilized, we repeat constantly, usually word for word, our standard rap on a subject. Soon a sense of helplessness descends on the listener because it's clear we are Johnny-one-notes. When the Parent has run its course, we've got no more to say. We are left only with repeating what we have already said. Refocusing the question or trying to shift the discussion will only turn on the tape again, to play what already has been said. Remember, a person who stays consistently in the Parent is not bad. He or she just doesn't function well and is using the Parent instead of the Adult. Still, the characteristic insistent behavior is not helpful. It is likely to downgrade conversation and weaken the social enterprise.

When the mind is not functioning and is closed to new data, the social fabric loses tensility. It tends to become conformist and brittle. People accept what's going down, seeking only comfort or escape from punishment. They live their lives at effect. Their motivation does not stem from internal conviction. In a conformist organization where differences are not valued, people lack integrity. Honesty is negotiable. If the day calls for dishonesty they'll do that as easily as being honest. For them, life springs from the avoidance of discomfort rather than from the creative life force. The sense of self is lost in aping others. Pleasure replaces joy and belief replaces knowledge.

Parent-dominant people live the reality they create in their heads. Skinner calls it "mentalism"—mistaking your perceptions for reality. Werner Erhard, observing this phenomenon, comments: "Most people live their lives as if their life didn't depend on it." It starts with a childhood fantasy: Wouldn't it be nice if all the brothers were brave and all the sisters virtuous? If evil skulked away from persistent virtue and a pot of gold awaited at the end of every rainbow? The fantasy slips easily from infant wishes to adolescent insistence that life be that way. We must pursue the Camelot vision. The man from La Mancha is a role model. Powerful and moving, the vision excites our Child and mobilizes our Parent. So romance displaces what's so, belief substitutes for experience, ritual replaces reality, and life becomes a soap opera. Parent energy makes us more rigid, more sterile, more dependent on the powers of others.

The way to decathect the power of the Parent is to test it with reality. The way to undermine its hold is to compare its content with what really is so. When Parent positionality is held up against reality, the Adult sees the difference and opts for reality. When the Adult queries the Parent, these are the questions it asks:

- What evidence (facts) do you adduce to support your prejudice?
- How did you arrive at your position?
- What are the consequences for others of your behavior?

- How do you relate what you say to be true here to other things you say to be true there?
- Who opposes your position?
- How is your position evolving? What do you expect to happen next?
- What other people support your position? What do they say are the imponderables?
- What assumptions do you travel on?

Dealing with these questions and their answers will move energy into the Adult. The Adult is potentially the most effective ego state and awaits only the opportunity to return control to the individual.

3. The content of the parent ego state is usually derived from the historical parents or parent surrogates. At a young and impressionable age we accept respected parents, friends, and teachers as role models. We attempt to please others by aping them. Below our level of awareness, we onload those things we admire in key others and seek to achieve their success. This material operates powerfully within us, usually without the mediation of the Adult. Thus people may accept a self-limiting script such as "You'll always be a no-good like your father" or "Short people never get the best jobs." More serious is the acceptance of self-destructive injunctions like "Don't think," "Get sick," and "Fail." People go about their lives under the control of what can aptly be called witch messages.

Fortunate are those who are scripted to be winners. Because their models are healthy and successful individuals, success seems easy and natural to them. They often appear not to have to struggle. It was never hard for them to accept such scripting messages as "You'll always be successful in love," "You're an achiever like your grandfather," and "You were born under a lucky star." Can such messages be corroborated in reality? This is the test of good Parent material.

4. The Parent ego state is functionally unable to take in new data and see people and things as they are. Life becomes a con game or series of stratagems. Unconsciousness reduces the options of others. They are either dragged into games and rackets or reduced to avoiding and resisting. This is the way unconsciousness spreads. When the Parent is cathected, the mind is blind. It can't take in new data. Each day is not fresh, vital, and new. It is a replay of infant days. That is not a metaphorical statement. It is a fact of the psyche. When people are on automatic, their behavior and mental processes are the consequences of past programming.

Time spent in the Parent is nongrowth time. If we don't take in new data and can't see things as they are, we're stuck. We've functionally stopped growing. Daily we are met with new challenges, relationships, and threats. If we don't see them for what they are, we don't have a prayer of solving them. If they are not challenges ripe with new hopes and opportunities, our ability to prevail is markedly reduced. When today's challenges are only repeats of age-old threats, we have doomed ourselves to failure.

When we are unable to decathect our Parent, moving energy into our Child and Adult, we are run by an engine so markedly inefficient it has little hope of position in a race. Parent is the source of one of the saddest things about human nature. Many of us never seem to learn. We run into a brick wall and fall down—and get up to run into it again. We do it until we no longer have the strength left to do anything except wonder about the futility of things and maybe, just maybe, about the significance of our behavior.

5. Selection, reduction, distortion, and projection are the mechanisms the Parent ego state uses to make sense of life. By selectively seeing and hearing only what already fits their preconceptions, Parent-dominant people approach life without challenge. "If I say a thing emphatically it's true" is the Alice

in Wonderland mentality of Parent types. Life has to be diminished and distorted to get into their heads. It must be reduced to their particular language, time, roots, and beliefs. It is impossible to cram life into a belief system. Parent works out a we and they, citizens and barbarians, male and female, good and bad schema to handle what it can't comprehend in a unified way. If Parent doesn't include you—ipso facto you're not worth including.

When people cast their own ideas, interpretations, and attitudes out on the world and then treat them as objective reality, this is projection. Experts agree perception may be 90 percent projection. We say of Parent-dominant workers, "They are in their heads." They believe their own soap operas. It is by projection that they keep their belief systems going.

Some interesting and surprising research has been done in this area. In the summer of 1971 Philip Zimbardo and associates set up a mock prison in the basement of Stanford University's psychology building.* From 75 volunteers a homogeneous sample of 20 "normal-average" college students was selected. By the flip of a coin half were assigned the role of guards, and the remainder were prisoners. The experiment, which was planned to run two weeks, had to be aborted after six days. By the end of the first day both sides had lost sight of the fact that they were in an artificial situation. They began to act as if it were objective reality. "Prisoners" became resigned; they began to feel powerless, hopeless, anonymous, and dehumanized. "Guards" became abusive and controlling and experienced feelings of power, superiority, strength, and control. A few, unable to take the authoritarian atmosphere, became depressed and left after the second day. Those who remained continued to view the situation as real life. As their behavior changed in response to the prison environment, so did their

---

* Philip Zimbardo, Craig Haney, and W. Curtis Banks, "A Pirandellian Prison," *The New York Times Magazine*, April 8, 1973.

attitudes. It was not the mock prison that controlled them, but the prison they created in their minds.

The U.S. Air Force reports losing a significant percentage of pilots during combat training against a mock aerial enemy. Overinvesting in the game some pilots lost sight of reality and crashed into the side of the mountain. They cathected Parent, went unconscious, and lost touch. They played a third-degree game.

Another fascinating piece of research was done by Stanley Milgram at Yale University in the early 1970s.* The experimental design was unique. A random sample of the population was invited to take turns as teacher in what purported to be an experiment in memory training using adverse stimuli. The so-called teacher would ask the subject to spell a word and, when the subject failed, would administer electric shocks of increasing intensity. The scale on the shock generator ranged from 15 to 450, with 255 designated as "intense," 315 "extreme," 375 "dangerous," and 435 "fatal."

The "victim" was played by a 31-year-old high school biology teacher who actually received no shocks. He acted out the responses appropriate for each voltage stage. At 75 volts he grunted and at 120 he shouted that the shocks were becoming painful. At 135 he shouted that he wanted to stop, and at 180 he cried out that he could not stand the pain. At 270 volts there was an agonized scream. At 300 he shouted in desperation and pounded on the wall. At 330 there was silence. The experimental results were so startling they are still hard to believe. All 40 "teachers" administered shocks above 300 volts and 26 reached the lethal range. The results differed somewhat under other experimental conditions, but always they were frighteningly similar.

The "teachers" saw in their minds a relationship with a sci-

* Stanley Milgram, *Obedience to Authority* (New York: Harper & Row, 1974).

entific organization and an "official" experimenter who quietly urged them to continue. Cathecting their Parent and dealing from their minds, they carried out violence against a protesting and harmless subject. With no energy in their Adult and Child, they gave up their reason and their humanity. Questions did not leap to their minds. They had no feelings available for the victim. They accepted their projection without testing it in reality.

The Parent ego state is powerfully implanted in us by our historical parents—the source of all life and its blessings. Not only do our parents give us biological life; they also give us our social life. This is awesome. Long before we have operable intelligence to test their beliefs, assumptions, and attitudes, they imprint their belief systems on our tapes. One of the reasons people easily accept derogations about themselves is that they are dependent on this Parent-Child mechanism. Parents taught us primarily by negative strokes, by making us feel wrong. Thus we tend automatically to accept as true negative things said about us. It is a faulty mechanism of the mind. It is not a question of reality. It's just how the mind works. We tend to believe things powerfully said and say things powerfully believed. It's the way our parents taught us.

All beliefs are wired with an antiremoval device. By some primordial sensing mechanism, the mind identifies a challenging idea and before thinking about what it might mean throws the baggage out. It does this by denial or avoidance. If the idea is presented again, the mind will distort it. Even if the idea is friendly or neutral, it will be viewed as an enemy and dismissed. If the new idea persists, the mind will deploy the heavy artillery. An attack will be made on the individual presenting the idea. Games will escalate in intensity. (See Chapter 10.)

Again, I talk about a mechanism of the mind. It is not a conscious thought process. Parent-dominant individuals are not wrong or bad. They are passive, not active. They are victims of what has been implanted in them. Some people experience this control mechanism as a voice in their head. The voice usually belongs to the key historical parent. The voice is often demanding and insistent, warning against certain choices even before they are consciously considered. Because the voice is not in touch with present reality, it is known as the "voice override." It overrides here-and-now possibilities.

The reason the voice override works so well is because we call on it so often. It is a constant source of protection, comfort, and satisfaction. It ties us back with our family for a number of generations. It literally defines who we are. We use it to select whom we will transact with, invite into games, and share our pastimes with. It's so much a part of us, we can no longer see it. The goal of behavior training is to make it visible so it comes under control of the Adult.

The Parent functions to keep itself on top. Everything outside either fits or is denied. The ability to see, hear, and feel things selectively is supported by worthy others. Those who count most with us also argue from the same distortions and projections. If we can make the world in our own image and if we have friends who conspire in agreement, that is enough for us. We no longer need to accept the rigors of seeing things as they are. It is more fun to see them as we wish them. Of course, this is a circular process that goes nowhere. People caught in this cycle have stopped growing.

GOALS OF PARENT REDUCTION

All behavior change takes place in a system where others reinforce accepted behavior or attempt by withholding rewards to extinguish what is considered unacceptable behavior. This is consonant with the hypothesis that behavior is largely a function of the environment and that to change behavior one must modify the culture in which it occurs. At the same time, people always remain responsible for their own behavior.

As workers become more sensitive to their ego states and more aware of the effect of their behavior on others, and as they see their role in contributing to larger systems change, they energize the change process. When they use their Adult awareness, group process and their own behavior become integral to what is being managed. Rather than being the effect of change, workers cause and manage it. As more workers accept the challange and its responsibilities, the organization moves toward critical mass. The scale of individual change is stretched to the point where transformation takes place. The company then operates on new assumptions with more powerful intelligence, and problems are understood more clearly.

The largest change people experience is a reduction of the Punishing Parent ego state in favor of the Child and Adult. This process is abetted by group action, but individual initiative is the primary source. Below is a list of benefits workers enjoy when their Parent tapes are decathected in favor of the Child and Adult. This reparenting process is known as empowering the personality.

1. *Return of control of self.* Rather than being under the control of the internalized historical parents, the person is returned to the here and now. The problems of recathecting the Child may be formidable. Not so for the Adult. When energized, the Adult can function full power immediately. It is not dependent on historical antecedents. Life then becomes a constant series of choices between positionality and reality, between Parent and Adult-Child. The new sense of self is a liberating experience that over time profoundly affects behavior.

2. *Discovery of the authentic self.* The authentic self is that which is us and no one else. It is the historical Child plus the consciousness substratum that all historical events are recorded onto. Discovery of the self usually comes later in a development program. It is part of level 4—motivational activities. To the degree we are socialized, we are like everybody

else. To the extent we are rational, we follow Aristotelian rules of logic like everyone else. It is the difference in our feeling structure and consciousness substratum that is us and no one else. The discovery of self always gives joy and is a source of power.

3. *Restoration of consciousness and intuition.* The shift from unconsciousness to consciousness is accompanied by a shift in perspective. Many workers report the world simply looks different to them. It seems clearer and more sensible. It is more fun. It is by intuition that we make our great leaps forward. When the Adult and Child work together, new insight is achieved. It usually comes in the form of a hunch, guess, belief, or fantasy and leaps full blown from the mind. "I wonder if a league of nations isn't the answer." "I believe that workers and management can work together 100 percent in powerful and supporting ways beneficial to all." "I believe we can end hunger in the world by the year 2000." Like Einstein's great leap of faith, all intuitive ideas have to be patiently and deliberately worked out. What insight conceives, effort makes real. Institutions that move us forward come out of a fertile and cultivated mind. They cannot be planned for, only welcomed.

4. *Release of natural energy.* It takes energy to maintain our prejudices in the face of fact. It takes energy to diminish and distort our perceptions of reality. It takes energy to keep our daily act going. When we give up making life over in our own image, we free a great amount of energy to invest in constructive effort. Much of the daily act we put on goes nowhere. When we give it up and opt for living our lives as they are, things get better. A life that is controlled by the Parent ego state has a dreadfully predictable quality. It is scripty, a soap opera. Getting off it invigorates the personality, as energy and awareness flow back into it.

5. *Improvement of operable intelligence.* This idea may seem to be grandiose. It is not. For many people, not knowing about the three ego states seems to disable their Adult, which be-

comes lost in the confusion of energies. Discovering the three ego states gives people an opportunity to separate them out and choose the one they wish to operate from in any given situation. Using available options is a function of the Adult. Each application of this new skill strengthens operable intelligence. No longer being compelled to use the Parent when the Child is appropriate is a form of heightened intelligence. Restoration of the Child ego state, with its intuitive powers, strengthens intelligence further. A fully functioning worker who has all this available is immensely powerful.

6. *Restoration of individual growth.* Related to the improvement of operable intelligence is the restoration of growth. One of the sad things about workers whose energy is lodged in the Parent is that their maturation has ceased. At some time in the past, their growth stopped. They became fixed at that point. When the Parent is decathected in favor of the Child or Adult, the potential for growth is restored. Workers again become open to new data from the world. Their perception changes. They see things as they are, not as others said they were. They can experience, possibly for the first time, life at first hand. They can test their old assumptions against reality and draw conclusions about how things are.

7. *Experience of joy.* Pleasure is derived from the material world. Joy comes from the direct experience of the self. Many workers report a new sense of self, energy, and power as they take back control of their lives from the old tapes in their heads. At bottom, joy is the discovery of new dimensions of the self, previously not available.

THE CHANGE PROCESS

Five steps are involved in the process of weakening the Parent and strengthening the Adult and Child.

1. *Building trust.* The first step is to build trust in the sys-

tem and its key members. Managers need to have enough initial faith in the program to commit themselves and their teams to development. A clear sense of self and its boundaries, a decontaminated Adult, a Natural Child with sufficient energy to complete the task, and a comprehensive theory are what managers need. They need a sense of protection, a sense that the organization is not going to fall apart when the horses of openness and change are let out of the barn.

2. *Reveal the program.* A new-style development program changes the nature of the organization. It does not seek to do a little more of what people are already doing—for example, being a little more honest, cooperative, or friendly. The program seeks to transform the company. It is based on a wholly new set of social assumptions. The purpose of a new-style development program is to transform the way workers and managers experience the company. When this happens, situations people have been trying to change or have been putting up with simply clear up.* And people don't have to try.

The goal of the program is to create a more integrated and productive organization. Company culture is the target of change. Emphasis is placed on replacing old-style structures, strategies, and assumptions with concepts more suitable to the postindustrial age. The movement is from bureaucratic to familial. The thrust of the effort is on solving contemporary business problems; at the same time skills of openness, trust, and collaboration are developed. The task is to make those problems of process, behavior, and motivation previously unseen, available to workers. When this happens, space is created for workers to train themselves. Workers won't be the same after taking part in such a program. There are no limits to human growth.

3. *Enlist others.* When entering a system, look for those al-

---

* This is a redaction of the basic purpose of est as stated by its founder, Werner Erhard, in an explanatory brochure.

ready using new-style strategies. Some members will be well advanced in the human sciences. Some will be temporarily stuck, needing only the impetus of the program to begin growing again. They are an important resource to any program, and their ready agreement and support are helpful. The majority, still under the control of the Parent, will experience differing levels of resistance and exhibit a variety of fight or flight behaviors. A few will prefer to live with their old stratagems. They will seek to avoid growth in a variety of ways.

Those who value the opportunity to stretch and grow become a natural cadre of leadership for transferring responsibility for growth to individual workers. Teachers offer people the opportunity to train themselves. They create a context of learning. The successful transference of creative initiative from the trainer to team members is an important bridge to cross. New-style development proceeds on the assumption that workers and managers are the resource of their own development. The handles to the doors of learning are all on the inside. Even when people are indifferent or resistant, they are the resource. Continually enlisting others in alignment is a measure of spreading change.

4. *Destabilize the system.* Change does not occur without stress. The system will ignore and hope to outlast the new style. A few cosmetic changes will be welcomed and applauded. Most will conspire to keep change away from home. There will be easy agreement: "He needs to change." The Parent ego state will assume: "I'm OK just the way I am." An unspoken conspiracy will be mounted to deny the symptoms and keep the sickness hidden. Innovation will be greeted with bemused tolerance. At some point energy needs to be expended that discomfits, upsets, and intrudes. Old allegiances, work habits, and games previously considered harmless may need to give way to new people, ideas, and processes. Some will consider the change solely directed at them and demand extra support.

Others will be fearful of the outcome and speak of losing their way. They will prefer the past.

Speaking the truth with love is one of the most difficult things we do. Confronting with clarity demands self-knowledge and self-control. Intrusive entrances into the organization are always for clear goals:

- To get workers off their acts.
- To encourage people to speak authentically and directly from where they are.
- To dislodge relationships based on status and role and foster ones based on knowledge, competence, and caring.
- To stimulate workers to take risks and begin committing 100 percent of their energies to their work and to the community.
- To interrupt games and replace them with authentic encounters.
- To enlarge the collective vision of the organization.
- To powerfully influence upstream and downstream units.

It takes energy to bring about this sort of change, energy that may cause conflict. Force always develops counterforce. Resistance will mount. Attempts will be made to discredit or discard the new program. People will remember the past with new affection. It will seem increasingly appealing when compared with present tension. People will warn: "It won't work." When the fight is past and won, the growth curve will turn up again. This disheartening period can be expected to repeat itself from time to time.

Learning is cumulative. Periods of tension cannot be avoided. Recently at lunch a superintendent excitedly said to me, "If you had spoken like that six months ago I would have understood you sooner." I had not changed my way of talking. He was simply seeing it from his new-style lens and suddenly it made sense to him. He was excited about his new insight and the potential it offered. Some things have to be experienced before others make sense.

5. *Support the system as it restabilizes.* A sailing ship is very ungainly when it comes about. It loses headway as the sails luff and then flap violently in the wind. The stays grow slack before shifting tension. The sheets run out. The blocks whine. The boom clumsily swings across the cockpit. It is a dangerous time in high seas. The crew, fearing a crosswind, watches intently as the bow swings over. A wave of relief sweeps over everyone as the craft gains momentum on a new tack.

The same is true for an organization in change. Once a new-style program is launched, those responsible can only wait as the organization points in a new way, gathers energy, and begins to make headway. At this time do not worry that change is slow. Warning away from obvious hazards, encouraging the fearful, adding to their store of knowledge, and handling any crises that may from time to time appear—these are the ways to stay with the system as it moves in a new direction.

Managers and workers in a development program face the problem of having to do many things at once. Old-style systems often are inefficient. They take too much energy to run. They can be hard on everybody. The additional challenge of process and behavior management will strain the system. This needs to be planned for. Nourishment and support must be available as workers clear the deadwood out of their relationships. A number of workers will stress themselves needlessly and may feel near the breaking point. Once they are free of self-limiting and scripty behavior, they will be surprised at how different things are. They will have available all the energy they need to accomplish work they previously thought far beyond their capacity.

What reactions will people have as the system encounters the challenge of change? Many workers will experience stress and discomfort. Those whose investment is high in things as they are will be especially distressed. They need to be supported as they go through it. It is the desire to escape discomfort that powers resistance to change. Workers need both the skills to handle upsets and the support to help them through the process. Those who have operated a long time on automatic have a low risk-taking quotient. Their ability to undertake new directions will be hampered by fears of failure. Large are the fears of those who have risked little. Whatever new benefits are to be gained by the new behavior, there will be some feelings of loss when the old has been set aside. This is the source of the bit of gallows humor: "They may only be worries, but they are mine and I'm used to them."

As new insight is brought to bear and people begin to realize the part they have played in the failures of the past, they often experience chagrin and guilt, with feelings of loss for what might have been. These barriers must be worked through. Taking responsibility for the shift in one's behavior from Parent to Adult-Child, from unconsciousness to consciousness, from old style to new style is in a sense a heroic act. It is not a task for "sometime patriots." It takes energy and perseverance. There are no shortcuts.

PROGRESSIVE RELAXATION RESPONSE

Upsets are a common problem. They tend to turn social transactions into games or fights. When people are upset, they usually exhibit either defeat or attack behavior. Wildly shifting behavior is another clue. An upset occurs when energy flows into the Not OK Child. Typically, people then mobilize the Parent for fight or flight. When energy flows out of the Adult, people are no longer able to maintain split attention. They go unconscious. In surrendering active control of their behavior to their Parent programming, they are in effect "running a rap," "being on it," or "going crazy."

People can free themselves from upsets by practicing progressive relaxation.* The goals of the progressive relaxation response are:

1. Identifying operant ego states.
2. Improving intelligence.
3. Reducing stress.
4. Releasing energy for work.
5. Practicing split attention.

Deep relaxation can be achieved in 15 minutes. First, with your eyes closed, focus your attention on the room about you. Be aware of what's there. (Eyes are closed for training to block out distracting visual stimuli. With practice, the exercise can be done with eyes open.) With closed-eye vision examine wall and furniture arrangements; light levels and shadow patterns; wall, floor, and ceiling dimensions; colors and textures; people's behavior and attitudes. As you do this, energy begins to flow into the Adult.

The second step in progressive relaxation is to tune into communication from your body. With eyes closed place your attention systematically on the muscles, joints, fascia, and organs of your body. If you discover tense or contracted muscles, relax them and keep them relaxed. If you sense cold or hot sweat, twitching, pain, or trembling, simply "observe" it. Allow yourself to experience these sensations and they will go away. It is a perfectly natural and easy process. It requires no discipline or effort. At the end of the second stage of progressive relaxation you will experience a deepening sense of restfulness.

The third step in progressive relaxation is to turn your attention to your consciousness. Do not reflect, make judgments, interrupt, or interfere. Do not initiate thought. Simply observe

---

* Herbert Benson, M.D., *The Relaxation Response* (New York: William Morrow and Company, 1975).

what comes up for you. Allow it to surface. What will come up will be opinions, remembered experiences, ideas, and a variety of feelings like fear, confusion, guilt, and pleasure. Do not attempt to deal with them. Observe them. What you allow yourself to experience disappears. What you avoid, deny, or repress you keep. If you keep packing in enough material, it will debilitate you. Your intelligence will clog and your intuition weaken.

Three things will probably surface in your consciousness. First, you will see things out of your immediate past experience. You will discover you heard, saw, understood, and experienced far more than you supposed. This will prove to be an important new source of data. Second, you will observe things you have been avoiding. Things for some reason you do not wish to deal with will be there just below your level of awareness. The barriers to releasing this material may be dimly visible. After you deal with the barriers, the material will surface. If you allow yourself to experience it, it will go away.

Restimulations from childhood will be a third level of experience. They are more than memories. You will experience the same joy, confusion, and fear you did then. Along with pictures will come feelings and judgments. When what you get is pleasant, enjoy. Whatever you get, allow it to surface. It will disappear. After you have experienced this material, you will be left with satisfaction. You will be in touch with yourself.

At this point you will find yourself in a state of deep relaxation. In this condition you will get more rest in 15 minutes than you would in eight hours of deep sleep. In this state you have available to you the vast uncluttered resources of your mind. Problems that before seemed insurmountable will return to chewable size. Relationships that have been failing will begin to clear. Your sense of self will be strengthened and you will experience your life as working again.

8

Team-Building
Work Groups

An important part of any development effort is the creation of
an opportunity for all workers to meet regularly around issues
of work life. This is particularly important for the hourly rated
workforce and is consonant with the recognized need to develop
all levels of the organization.

When we talk about improving a company, what we really
mean is developing the workforce—or, to be more precise,
creating opportunities for workers to develop themselves.
Workers are the resource. They are the insight, the energy—
both means and ends. An organization can't grow if its people
don't grow. As I see it, development of workers is management's central task. Change seems to be coming toward us at
an increasing rate of speed. Things are going to be different.
Change is inevitable and has major impact on the workforce. In
a new-style development program, management seeks by controlling this powerful force to direct it rather than be its victim.

Although change takes many faces, increasing competition
in the marketplace is the most compelling change in modern
life. Competition for resources, energy, market share, and
technological advances is not going to ease up. An annual 10
percent increase in company productivity is needed just to stay

even with inflation. The need to increase product quality and production efficiency never diminishes. We have gone far in improving marketing techniques, personnel practices, wage and salary policies, and the like. No longer is there any doubt that the people who do the work are the key to the whole thing. It is in empowering workers that the great gains of the future are to be made.

The concept of team building applies to work those principles of democracy that made America great. Democracy means, not bureaucratic concern for status, roles, and rituals but developing families of workers committed to achieving common goals and to supplying mutual support and protection. Democracy is never a finished product. It is an evolving system to which citizens contribute by continued and responsible social action. As workers daily solve problems, enhance their own self-esteem, and contribute to increased productivity, they are continually voting for democracy. Team-building groups produce better citizens and enhance the commonweal.

My recent experience training groups in Europe and Central America revealed a deeply rooted worker frustration that sought redress in radical politics, including terrorism. Such frustration gives incentive to our efforts. The supposedly inevitable hostility between labor and management is not only wrong but wrongheaded. We have repeatedly demonstrated the error of the Marxian dialectic. The conflict is not between socialism and capitalism, but between old style and new style. It is between bureaucratic and familial systems.

Work groups are primarily results oriented. Team members join together to analyze and solve work problems and at the same time discuss relevant group process and behavior issues. Observation of a large number of team-building groups makes clear that real worker-directed change takes place. There are clear differences in attitudes and behavior before and after work groups have been functioning for some time. Some of the more obvious changes are listed in Table 3.

Table 3. Impact of team building on worker behavior.

Before	After
"Nothing changes around here. It will always be the same."	Problems get solved. As time goes on bigger issues are faced and resolved.
Energy is spent on beating the "system." There are high grievances and absenteeism, lost tools and time, spoilage and waste.	Workers have a sense of "ownership" of company goals and membership in a family team playing the game 100 percent.
People feel unimportant, with a diminished sense of self-worth.	Workers feel increasing sense of OK, with marked reduction in anger.
Performance appraisal is just another way to punish and control.	Work group sets goals, monitors results, and makes midcourse corrections. Members are mutually supportive and share learning.
"Being here is stressful and depleting; that is how I know it is work."	Work is an occasion for self-expression, social contribution, and pleasure.
"Nobody cares about me or how I work. I'm only told when I do something wrong."	Communication on business issues is easy and open. Coaching is regular and supportive. Nurturing behavior becomes normative.
"This place makes no sense to me."	As employees are given opportunities to tell the truth, work life becomes increasingly meaningful.
Management is the all-powerful enemy.	Managers have their responsibilities like all of us. They can be counted on to do the best for the company.
People don't talk to each other or listen to each other.	Employees identify and use each other's resources. They are willing to influence each other and superiors.

When an old-style, impersonal bureaucratic organization concerned with rank and prerogatives moves toward a more integrated system focused on problem solving and supporting relationships, it causes some management worry. Managers who have achieved their present status with old-style behavior become reluctant to try new ideas that call for behavior change. Those unable or unwilling to change usually find it easier to select themselves out, seeking more traditional organizations. Those willing, even eager, to change need consistent and careful support. The willingness to tell the truth about problems and process in one's work life will also affect one's family and community life. The changes are almost all positive, but no change occurs without some stress.

When problem solving is pushed downward and team building takes place among hourly rated employees, some middle managers may see themselves as redundant. When human resources cease to be wasted and the system becomes open, those whose task was communication and coordination may think of themselves as excess baggage. However, when the organization focuses, really focuses, on problems, the excess will be more apparent than real. Organizations don't want for problems. There are more than enough to go around. What we need is increased clarity, sharper priorities, and retraining. For those committed to their own growth, this can be a restorative process. Employees who have been marking time or shuffling papers can return to the hard growing edge.

Many managers fear that if they adopt a collaborative style, they will lose some of their power. This is not so. When people who seek to appear powerful are secretive and behave defensively, everyone has less power. Under old-style approaches there was just less power available for everyone. Power is information and competency. When these are shared openly, everyone has more power. In a new-style company power flows upward. Even senior officials have more. During World War II American combat teams were astonishingly effective because of their depth of leadership. When a senior officer was removed, a subordinate quickly took over and unit effectiveness was little diminished.

Rule: Do not ask workers to tell you the truth if you have any doubts about your willingness to do something about what they say. This is fundamental. The decision to be open and square with your employees needs to be carefully made and remade throughout the development effort. It is even more important when considering work groups. The goal of work groups is to create space for workers to cooperate and to define and solve work problems. Integrity demands that if you set up groups you commit yourself to listening actively and responding. Some things groups cannot appropriately work on. They include legal, design, patent, marketing, and new product matters. This can be made clear from the beginning. Managers who use work groups are almost always surprised at how effective they are.

Out of my experience with work teams, I believe the following conditions are prerequisite to a successful program.

1. The group meets to identify, analyze, and solve business problems. If resolution of a problem involves other levels and departments, the group should make recommendations to the appropriate authority. To repeat: Work groups do not merely point out problems for others to solve. They are themselves part of the solution. Because they have undervalued themselves for a long time and been underutilized by the organization, workers may join the group expecting only a bull session. It takes time for them to adjust to the discovery that they are seen as responsible, able, and desirous of contributing to company success. Patience and clear discussion will overcome initial confusion and resistance.

2. Groups work on their process and behavior issues as they meet to solve problems. Shifting from an authority-obedient environment to one where men and women work together powerfully and cooperatively involves discovery and change on

everybody's part. With the four-step development model, change becomes transformation. This takes plenty of support from supervisors plus a willingness to encourage provisional attempts and to tolerate false starts.

3. Training is a necessary component of all development programs. It can be done in a variety of ways and usually has two phases: (1) technological instruction on the machinery and the job plus problem-solving techniques, including financial ratios; and (2) training on the assumptions, strategies, and skills of new-style companies. These two training tracks are often referred to as technical and management training, or "can do" and "will do" factors.

4. Participation in work groups must be voluntary. Workers have a right not to take part. Even so, only a few initially resist. Since real work issues are discussed, most do not want to be left out. The group is where the action is. When nurturance and concern become part of the process, the desire to join increases. Infrequently workers select themselves out via transfer or resignation. Presumably for some, it is easier to change jobs than to take responsibility for their own growth.

Members who at first are suspicious and withholding soon enter a period of discharging, when they unload their long- and short-term frustrations. After this they begin a cautious exploration of how the group is going to function. What is the cost of admission? Who is going to lead? In about six months they will find themselves working vigorously on production and quality problems. After nine months or so they will move on to problems related to team life, including absenteeism, alcoholism, and other behavior problems. At each stage management is standing by to supply the training insight needed to unblock the group's development.

Ordinarily, groups are led by their supervisor. If managers or supervisors resist joining, a different set of problems arises. It is not a happy situation and probably indicates deeper underlying problems. With the program coordinator's help, the group can elect its own leadership and proceed. The coordinator must keep communication channels open to relieve pressure and ensure that misconceptions do not arise. Successfully functioning groups strongly influence neighboring operations both upstream and downstream. Supervisors have started groups despite resistance from managers.

Job security is the primary concern of workers. They see spreading the work, not breaking the rate, as in their own best interests. Generally, they consider the success or failure of the organization as someone else's concern. This particularly makes sense if workers feel that management is indifferent to their lives. Such a perception is a major cause of America's lowering productivity compared with Japan and West Germany. Any effort to increase productivity is likely to be met with resistance, since common sense suggests that increased production can lead to layoffs. Arguments about the increased ability of the company to compete in the marketplace and national pride are likely to fall on deaf ears.

A new-style development program usually starts at the top and cascades down through the organization. Once hourly rated employees hear of the program they usually welcome involvement. Management's position is "We don't ask workers to face challenges we have not resolved ourselves." Developing a system of job security—many companies now have them—could be one of the first tasks that teams work on. If market conditions mandate production cutbacks, the extra time could be spent working on process modifications, increased training, and maintenance. In West Germany during periods of decreased production, companies have found it useful to share workers among themselves. When there is openness, trust, and collaboration, no problem is impervious to determined effort.

If managers have not had experience in team building, they may have serious doubts about the program that prevent them from moving ahead. Not knowing the outcome in advance, they worry about which direction change may go. Unwilling to threaten union security, they worry about possible union intransigence. Unsure about their workers' attitudes and feelings, they worry about a cynical or disinterested response. Well-planned and thoughtfully executed team building of work groups has always made things go better. It is commonplace now: Workers support what they help to create.

Team building presumes that senior management understands and accepts responsibility for the life of the groups. Work groups can be made part of the company business plan. Development of group leadership skills can be made part of a management development program. Managers who make themselves available to work groups on request enhance motivation and may be called upon frequently to help groups solve technical problems. Over time, groups seek to tackle increasingly complex problems. Management needs to deliberate carefully before denying a problem to a work group.

In one company work groups that had successfully taken responsibility for scheduling, manning, and quality control wanted more influence over rates. Division leaders, impressed with the groups' competence, stood ready. They ran into resistance at the corporate level. After arduous debate, the division leaders won concessions for a trial. Today, two years later, all wage and salary matters in the division are open. Salary ranges and wage rates are published. Work teams influence decisions related to their own budgets.

STRUCTURE OF WORK GROUPS

In building work groups, there are three levels of structure that need to be considered: (1) group membership, (2) supervisory leadership, and (3) plant coordinator. Sometimes a fourth level arises: (4) the plant steering committee. Let's consider these independently.

1. *Group membership.* Who should be members of the group

is not always an easy question. The organization chart may not be helpful. Natural work groups are composed of people who work face to face regularly and are dependent on one another. They may report to the same supervisor. Generally, anyone who desires to contribute to the resolution of problems should be a member. The best way to form a group is to let workers volunteer. This way, the natural relationships within the organization will work for you. I have not had success creating groups composed of a variety of individuals like planners, schedulers, engineers, and pipefitters—probably because they are cross-grained with the formal and informal organizations already in place. Groups can co-opt such special help as they need from time to time. This is an opportunity to learn how to ask for and receive helpful help.

What can happen when people get together to discuss and work on problems is revealed in the following history. In some consumer product lines, packaging is a significant contribution to expense. In a Midwestern plant, four high-speed machines packaged a confection. They were operated by teams of five women. When a machine went out of sync, wrappers would come out skewed. Usually 10 to 12 cartons were filled before the error was caught. The products were shipped abroad as seconds or sold to the armed forces.

When a machine misfired the following sequence of events took place. The twisted wrappers were discovered and an operator called the supervisor, who inspected the damage and stopped the machine. A maintenance engineer was summoned. When he arrived the trouble was reported, he repaired it, and tested the machine with a slow-paced trial run. He turned the machine back to the supervisor and then wrote up a machine status report. It was a rare day when a machine didn't go down at least once.

The members of the work team discussed the problem and came up with a more expeditious solution. Operators knew when a malfunction was taking place because of a change in the sound of the high-speed machine. They stopped the machine and, with a small set of tools provided them, made the adjustments they had seen maintenance make many times before. They conducted their own trials and reinstituted high-speed runs. Operators reported downtime only after the machine was fixed and called maintenance only when a major problem occurred. The saving in machine downtime was just over $400,000 in the first year. There was marked improvement in machine operators' morale.

2. *Supervisory leadership.* Work groups are usually led by the supervisor or foreman. The productivity of the group is largely dependent on the skill of this leader. The best leaders have their Child ego state fully available and can comfortably give authentic strokes. With their liberated Adult they gently restrain their own and others' Punishing Parent behavior. The most competent supervisors often consult with and support new group leader trainees. In large companies where multiple teams are doing the same work, stellar group leaders may be used to start up new groups. Groups can function without supervisory leadership, but usually not well. The supervisory leader has three main responsibilities:

- Overseeing group operations, including maintenance of productivity and good process.
- Providing group training on process, behavior, and work issues.
- Coordinating reports to and from other groups and higher management and securing technical consultants when needed.

3. *Plant coordinator.* The plant (section, division) coordinator, usually a dynamic member of the Personnel Department, is responsible for administering the program. Organized plants often find it useful to appoint two coordinators—one union and one management—who are jointly responsible for planning, scheduling, and decision making. If there is only one

coordinator, he or she may be overwhelmed with a variety of business and process problems. If you ask workers to tell you the truth, they will. A whole new set of issues is likely to arise, demanding candor, hard work, and inventiveness. The coordinator's support from topside has to be complete. He or she may have to confront managers who are not responding to initiatives from below or haven't taken responsibility for their group's process or their own behavior.

Many organizations find it useful to obtain outside consultant support in the initial stages of a development program. When building a contract with external consultants, you should keep three things in mind:

- Be clear about objectives of the program and the goals you expect consultants to achieve.
- Don't surrender power to consultants. Avoid all those games in the "Gee, You're Wonderful, Professor" category. It won't work for either party.
- Consultants are by definition temporary employees. From time to time discuss this point openly. Begin to face the problem of separation long before it happens.

The coordinator is the chief trainer, counselor, and confronter. By direct and indirect, formal and informal means, he or she assists those taking responsibility for change. The coordinator is the transfer point, providing the necessary skills, information, and coordination to enable groups to do their work expeditiously and effectively. The coordinator also ties the program to the rest of the organization through reports, notices of meetings, and the like.

4. *Steering committee.* As the program matures another support structure may appear—a steering committee. The committee may include both union and management trainers and coordinators, group leaders, department managers, and possibly technical staff (accountants, materials and machine engineers, and so on). The steering committee's meetings, often

held biweekly, offer an opportunity to report findings to the group. In order for leaders and trainers to receive the guidance, direction, and recognition they need, the committee must formulate policy and support new objectives in production, quality, safety standards, vendor relations, and the like. The impetus for work-related changes comes from the work groups themselves. The steering committee should not usurp workers' initiative and begin telling them what to do. Its task is to enable work groups to function more powerfully. Empowering work groups is the focus of the committee's deliberations.

In an organized plant, unions should be brought into the planning at the earliest stage. Unions recognize that workers are motivated to solve work-related problems and to win recognition through achievement. If the work improvement effort is candid and does not lead to layoffs, and if benefits are passed along to the workers, you can expect hearty union participation.

If the union is not brought in at the outset and does not take an active role in planning and decision making, the likelihood of the program's success declines sharply. The union cannot be expected to abrogate its primary role of protecting workers and securing for them better wages, hours, and conditions. Both parties need to agree at the outset that team-building sessions will not discuss issues covered by the contract or supplant the grievance process. Team building is possible when both sides recognize that they have a broader commitment to improving the quality of work life. The goal is to create space for workers to express more initiative and responsibility around work issues. For such an effort to be successful, all parties must cooperate.

Inviting union participation is based on certain new-style assumptions about contemporary labor-management relations.

- Labor and management have a common interest in the company's productivity and its ability to maintain a competitive edge in rapidly changing world markets.

- While maintaining their contractual rights secured through collective bargaining, unions are finding new areas for making common cause with management. In each case they must win the support of their membership.
- By participating in the design and implementation of work groups, the union is expanding its influence.

There are always suspicions when traditional adversaries develop a collaborative relationship. Fears about union security are best met by ensuring that unions have an equal role in designing and carrying out the program. Unions are fully able to assess the value of the program, both short and long term, from their traditionally protective posture. Further, they will be in a position to insist that not all new economic gains flow directly through to profits without concomitant benefits for the workforce. Union participation will reduce resistance and facilitate the transfer of learning to other units.

GROUP TRAINING AND GOALS

In the beginning, work group meetings are usually held biweekly, for 60 minutes. They may be held at the end or the beginning of the shift, depending on work flow. Pre- or post-shift meetings may be scheduled at a negotiated rate. Later, depending on the problems being worked on, meetings may be held weekly or even daily for short periods. The first three or four meetings will largely involve explaining the philosophy and goals of the new-style development program. The group leader conducts these initial meetings with the coordinator's assistance. As an alternative, training may be conducted with larger groups at the company training center before work group meetings begin.

Training includes an explanation of the change model, collaborative strategies, nurturing behavior, and Transactional Analysis and covers problem identification, analysis, and resolution. There are significant side benefits to team building. Workers claim it helps them conduct their family and community affairs more effectively. Working with groups that are able to manage process, give positive strokes, and set realistic goals can be an exhilarating experience.

Setting unmeasurable and unobtainable goals is a major source of worker frustration. The leader must ensure that specific and believable goals are set. One way is to set a large objective like the reduction of waste and then work on subgoals one at a time. Another way is to build an agenda of items workers wish to resolve, set priorities, and work from the top of the list. Still another approach is to isolate workable issues through force-field analysis. Under this approach, a basic issue is found—for example, "What makes this section more cost-effective?" Then those forces that promote cost-effectiveness are listed against those that restrain it. The group should keep in mind that it is sometimes more efficient to reduce restraining forces than to increase driving forces. A problem list is then developed for workers to resolve.

Developing a social contract is an important technique. Social contracting is based on the idea that workers have tacit agreements with each other on what is and is not acceptable behavior. When people understand this, they can discuss the agreements openly and make changes if necessary. Social contracting helps to ensure that members' expectations are met, that openness and mistakes will not be punished, and that members will not be underutilized. Workers are asked to respond to several questions, first in writing—to encourage clear thinking—and then orally before the group.

1. What do I want to receive from this group?
2. What do I not want to receive?
3. What do I want to contribute to this group?
4. What do I not want to contribute?

Contracting should take place at one of the earliest meetings. It has a salutary effect on workers' sense of self, others, and group membership. It is important the leader allow each member to state fully what is on his or her mind. Doubtless many members will want to discharge old frustrations and pains. Allow them to air their compaints fully so they can be free of them. Later remind them of the rule "Never complain to anyone who can't help you solve the problem—except once." Everyone gets an absolutely free and unrestrained bitch. After that he or she must get on with problem solving. Leaders should be taught how to identify and interrupt games so they can assist workers in freeing themselves from self-imposed rackets. Workers themselves will soon recognize the old chestnuts: "If It Weren't for Them," "Gotcha," and "Ain't It Awful" (see Chapter 10).*

Social life doesn't work if people break their contracts. Workers who have lived at the effect of others will experience stress when they are first asked to take responsibility for themselves and their group. This can be a source of frustration and potential failure. Group members can take responsibility for keeping their contracts with one another. It is the coordinator's responsibility to see that the company keeps faith with the workers. Since workers are at a critical stage of development on this issue, they will be supersensitive to management's failure to do what they intend.

Research demonstrates that when a task is quantifiable, a group can outperform any individual member a statistically significant number of times. Three variables are controlling: (1) the number of individuals contributing to the solution, (2) the group's knowledge of the subject under discussion, and (3)

---

* For a full explanation of games business people play, consult Dudley Bennett, *TA and the Manager* (New York: AMACOM, 1976), Chapter 9.

the quality of the process the group uses as it moves toward resolution. The optimal group size for problem solving is 10 or 15. Less than that is not adequate enrichment. More than that is unwieldy. In regard to group process, one type of group behavior undermines the effectiveness of group decision making more than any others. The phenomenon is called convergent thinking. In any work group powerful forces operate to bring about conformity. In group decision making it is vitally important to protect dissent. Norms and practices should be established at the beginning to encourage people to explore the unusual, innovative, and untried. All explorative attempts must be kept free from censure and criticism. If we are to improve group problem solving, dissent will have to be given free rein. This means developing the intuitive capabilities of workers. It is out of these that truly significant advances come. The chaos that many managers fear will result from untrammeled discussion seldom happens when members accept responsibility for group process and their own behavior.

QUESTIONS AND ANSWERS

Below are some common questions managers ask when considering a team-building program for hourly rated employees:

QUESTION Are there specific steps to follow in setting up a program?

ANSWER There are some obvious first steps that need to be taken, like securing management's informed approval, setting up a responsible labor-management committee, choosing a consultant or coordinator, and training leadership. However, the plan for each company is likely to be different. The program is not an appliqué that can be laid on all situations.

Some things are fundamental. Always focus on solvable

problems. Let people enjoy the good feeling of resolving their own work issues. Keep the program flexible. Keep it open to influence by those involved. Keep it dynamic. Discuss and resolve problems and misunderstandings as they arise. Don't allow them to fester beneath the surface, building up discontent. Face and tackle problems as soon as they become visible.

QUESTION   What is the most important precondition to success?

ANSWER   Management needs to actively support new-style management. Understanding it and believing it are not enough. Managers must also practice it and take responsibility for their own growth. It is not enough to train workers in behavior, communication, and decision-making skills. They need immediate opportunities to use these skills to solve problems on the job. Management will be most successful if it seriously supports all attempts by workers to take responsibility for their own jobs. Keeping lines of communication open across the organization, plus nurturing with positive strokes, will do much to bring good results.

Sometimes the program will reveal that managers are not wholly competent to do their jobs. If they are not old-style resistant, this just becomes another problem to be solved. Everyone has room to grow. When people get over being self-conscious and defensive about their flatsides, the resources of others become available to them. The ability to be open and to build trust is the real test.

QUESTION   Isn't team building among workers just another way to increase the rate?

ANSWER   If management is cynical about new style and is using the development program as a slicker way to control when people are not looking—that will soon be known. Many things will expose their act if they aren't willing to be open, tell the truth, and solve problems.

A development program will produce significant gains for

the company in productivity, quality, and innovation. Moreover, scrap loss, grievances, and absenteeism will go down. These things are intended to happen. They are the consequence of creating a more powerful organization where workers play the game 100 percent. What increased profits mean to workers and managers will have to be worked out between them. This is the time when people learn what capitalism is all about and discover why no other economic system is in its league.

QUESTION   What happens after the program is over?

ANSWER   Transformation is an ongoing process. There are no practical limits to individual and organizational development because there are no limits to the problems that come up. Problems are opportunities. That's not just pious flapdoodle. Once workers have taken responsibility for their own growth and the system has internalized its own development—it will just work.

Team building is not a program that has a beginning and an end. When critical mass is reached it becomes self-generating. An annual check on the teams and their leadership will help to keep them out of games and politics. Hiring procedures will, of course, include assessing the individual's ability to function in a familial organization. The orientation program will also stress new-style values.

9

Work Injustice

Some workers may be laboring daily and under conditions seriously detrimental to their health—physical, emotional, and social. Each day for them brings a debilitating level of stress that can only be endured. Work life is a progressive enfeeblement of the worker. All motivational aspects of work have been ignored. The worker is left alone to cope as best he or she can. Unfortunately, for relief workers often turn to the narcosis of alcohol or drugs. Work injustice is often hard to see because it is woven into the fabric of society. Those who share the same social structuring are predisposed not to see the destructive aspects of old-style workplaces.

Today we have enough new-style experience and knowledge to understand those situations that are unneccessarily abusive to workers. There are usually some work situations in every company that for a variety of reasons have not yet been humanized. Sometimes they occur within an otherwise new-style organization. Standards in an incentive shop are drawn too tight or a wage and salary program discriminates against certain workers. Power has been denied a group so that it is unable to solve its problems. A marginal supervisor who oppresses workers is tolerated. These situations may have occurred for complex historical and technical reasons. Often they are hard to talk about because people have an investment in things as they are and feel uncomfortable with a suggestion of change.

Work injustice is as lamentable as any other oppressive condition over which the victim has no control. Eliminating work injustice is a concern of everyone. Such injustice is the product of a work environment that steadily erodes the employee's ability to appropriately use the Parent, Adult, and Child ego states. Test for work injustice by asking: Are workers being confirmed in their moral lives? Are they being given opportunities to learn more about their work and the company? Do they have space to enter into supportive relationships? Work that deadens workers' ability to use their Child and enter into mutually supportive relationships needs to be changed.

In a West Coast manufacturing plant a group of women workers on assembly rails were known as barracudas. Their behavior reflected their scripting. They harassed each other continually and hazed new employees who were attempting to learn the process. When managers described the situation, their laughter had a gallows ring. No serious manager could look upon it without a feeling of disquiet. When work in effect becomes an attack on the value system of the larger community, it needs rethinking. Encouraging rapacious behavior in workers is an example.

Union organizers' main argument regarding work injustice is essentially a moral one. They maintain that management has demonstrated it does not value workers and will tolerate their abuse. "Just sign this authorization card," the unions entice, "and we assure you they'll listen to us. We will set things right for you." If the company does not promote human values, the unions stand ready to provide them. "Let us represent you and we will teach them to respect you, establish your job security, and give you a way to resolve your problems through a grievance-arbitration system." Often unions do just that.

The deterioration of the worker's ability to think clearly and solve problems is an unacceptable consequence of work injustice. Some Americans believe that working-class people are neither able nor willing to put forth the effort to develop themselves. "They are animals," some say. This view is both cynical and self-serving. The assumptions built into our democratic political system—the individual's ability to accept discipline, assess alternatives, and share in decision making—hold no less true for business. New-style management is high on workers. Its basic assumption is that the individual worker is our greatest asset. Workers share in human elegance. Though they may be unskilled and undermotivated, we do not jump to the erroneous conclusion they are essentially inadequate. Repeatedly across the country—in dog food, corrugating, packaging, and assembly plants as well as in banks and retail stores—development programs have been startlingly successful. When workers are given access to problems with responsibility and are recognized for their efforts, misanthropic ideas melt away. We are not dissuaded from this position by failure. If you start with cynical assumptions about companies and workers, you will arrive at a tortured idea of what work is all about. Cynical ideas are self-perpetuating.

The task is not to change people. People are perfectly all right the way they are. The task is not to motivate people. People are inherently self-starting. The task is to remove those things that demotivate them, to get out of their way. More precisely, it is to create the kinds of organizational structures that allow workers to get at problems and act in more independent ways so they can develop skill in solving problems on the job. True, many jobs do not offer much growth opportunity. But experience teaches us there is more room for innovation than old-style managers are apt to believe. The potential for greater achievement, recognition, and promotion increases when workers are retrained and given wider responsibility.

We often fly in the face of traditional assumptions about

people and work. Traditionally work arrangements are built around machinery. People are hired who can best function as adjuncts to machines. Sometimes they work alongside robots. Many industrial engineers would rather work with the certainty of machines than the uncertainty of workers. Our starting point is that along with work flow and machinery, the consequences for social systems must be factored in. This is a complex matter that includes space arrangements, workloads, noise levels, safety standards, and wage and salary administration. It is an idea whose time has come. In the past half-dozen years, work plus human plus architectural systems are being integrated by forward-looking management. Only in its infancy, this idea still needs development.

If the task is not to change people, what can we do with the underproductive and demotivated worker? Two things primarily. First, we create and publish the company's management philosophy on work issues. We create a context. By a variety of means, the elements of a company policy are made clear so each employee can translate them into action. Company philosophy includes business purpose, responsibilities to society, quality standards, company attitude toward workers and outsiders (vendors, distributors, and retailers), company policy on competition, profits, employee training, and desired behavior and attitudes.

Matsushita Electric Corporation has demonstrated for the world the catalytic role of management philosophy in company integration, productivity, and profitability. The company started from scratch after World War II and by 1976 had $5.8 billion in sales. Every company has its assumptions and principles, even if these are not explicitly stated. They are probably a potpourri of ideas, positive and negative, held below the level of management and worker awareness. Matsushita has constructed a power-giving set of principles and made them an explicit element of management strategy.

The company's primary principle is to make a positive contribution to humanity. It follows that the company seeks the greatest contribution from each worker. Management emphasizes the personal and professional growth of all employees. By urging people to make the most of themselves and by fostering a work environment in which an individual's job becomes a primary source of self-development and self-esteem, Matsushita has created a miracle for 83,000 employees in almost 200 plants in 130 countries.

The goal of a new-style development program is not to change employees but to create the opportunity for them to accept new challenges, try new behaviors, and stretch their attitudes about themselves and others. The percentage of those unwilling or unable to respond is miniscule. Most workers, when adequately trained and supported, go for new opportunities like trout for a black fly. The results, while often not those expected, are always greater than anticipated. By and large, workers welcome the chance to grow and accept new challenges. Creating the space that makes it possible is fundamental to new-style management.

Because work injustice is hard to see, it is hard to reduce. Injustice sets off a spiral motion downward. Negative assumptions create self-inhibiting organizations that stimulate self-limiting behavior which reinforces the original cynicism. The whole thing devolves tighter and tighter until we are left with a tough social mass that is inaccessible to reason. Not an uncommon phenomenon in political life, it has particularly painful consequences in business. At some point in the process companies may go completely out of control. Nobody understands what's happening. Nobody can summon the power necessary to bring about change. And finally nobody gives a damn. When that happens managers are left only with the option of resigning or "getting their own" while things go from bad to worse and the company is managed into the ground. A sad spectacle.

SELF-DEFEATING CULTURE

What are the elements of a self-defeating culture, and how do they reinforce each other? As a result of their historical parenting, lack of successful social experience, and residual Not OK feelings, most workers have a diminished opinion of themselves. Most, at some level, tend to believe the negative things said about them. They accept negative opinions as congruent with their own bad feelings, and as explanations of why others treat them so poorly. Behavior training equips the workers to unhook old bad feelings and develop a more realistic view of their skills and potential.

Since most workers' social experiences have been old style, there has been little opportunity for truly authentic game-free relationships. This in part explains why stroke starvation is common today. Family, school, business, military, and church encompass the social experiences of most people. These are largely power-on systems whose assumptions do not call forth maximum individual responsibility and group interdependence.

Few workers have a realistic view of the importance of their work in the scheme of things and the necessity of doing it supremely well. Having been in Parent-Child organizations all their lives, they are most comfortable when they are dominated and are following the orders of others. They experience distress when they are invited to act on their own or in cooperation with others. Having no positive experience of autonomy, they too quickly ask: "Who's going to tell us what to do?" They consider themselves lucky when they are secure in another person's schemes. Indeed, they may pride themselves on years of faithful servitude. Because of lifelong experiences in old-style organizations, they are ill-equipped to act in innovative ways when the situation demands it. This phenomenon is visible at all levels of the organization.

In my experience, the majority of managers would shield

long-term workers if they proved unable to cope with new work techniques. Lateral transfers, promotions, and demotions are sought as alternatives to company capital punishment—firing. When presented with a faltering employee, few managers will insist the only course is to replace the employee with a younger person. Almost none see the inevitable daily entropy of employee skills or use training to negate it. Training, retraining, and cross-training are new-style management's way of ensuring that workers remain current in a period of rapid change.

By and large managers have not been optimistic about human endeavor. They claim history to be on their side when they posit a variety of assumptions about native human aggression. Study and experience cause us to reject the widespread myth that people possess an innate belligerence. Human behavior is not so simple or narrow as other forms of life seem to be. Not limited by genetic structuring, with wider options, people are able to fashion fresh and unique responses to contemporary events. "Territoriality," "total depravity," "naked ape," and "the hunting hypothesis" do not adequately explain social life in the age of technology.

Some animals protect their "territory"—their food, nesting, and reproductive areas. Many animals meet these challenges over a vast area or migrate. Birds may defend one piece of real estate in which the male attracts and courts the female and then move into another area to nest and rear young. Intruders are met with a display intended to drive them off. This is ritual fight. It is clearly nature's idea that the biologically fitter of two opponents, by the clarity of his response, will win without ever suffering physical damage. Aggression is not innate in either the animal or human order. Only under rare circumstances will the competitive display result in harm to another.

Learning among humans replaces the mock battles of the lower orders. An ironical twist appears. Human beings are essentially social and cultural animals. They are defined not by genetic inheritance but by the ability to acquire culture through adaptation and learning. In fact, human behavior is extraordinarily sensitive to the environment. It is surprising how quickly workers who move from one company to another will clothe themselves in the attitudes, values, and behavior of the new organization. It does not matter how different the second was from the first.

The cooperative nature of people explains much more about the contemporary social predicament than does their predatory behavior. They are more like sheep than wolves. It is not their ferocity but their penchant to go along, to cooperate, to stand side by side that accounts for their destructiveness. A special kind of desensitizing training is necessary before they are capable of combat. A great many can be led by only a few to engage in destructive behavior—destructive, that is, to their own lives. This deeply rooted urge to belong and go along plus advanced weaponry makes modern wars unique in their destructiveness.

Our ascendant position in the natural order is based on our capacity for learning. Human beings can fashion limitless responses to challenges, and their communication with others greatly enhances their inventiveness. People are cultural animals who create social structures with values, roles, ways of making decisions, and rites of entrance and exit. Their social inventiveness—we call it process management—is now being put to the test of creating processes more rational and less threatening to the species.

Workers in old-style systems spend great amounts of effort milling around or engaged in games and politics, learning almost nothing to aid them in definition and resolution. Old-style workers continually look upward for guidance or at least for relief from a crisis. This is the natural consequence of old-style strategies, to be sure. Unable to stand alone, resist, innovate, or take risks, workers create nothing for superiors to manage. They go down with what they shouldn't.

The spiral movement downward proceeds on the following course. Workers in old-style systems gain little sense of self-worth from their work. This is reinforced by their residual Not OK feelings. They expect work to be painful. By definition if it were fun it couldn't be work. This idea is deeply rooted in our past. In the Book of Genesis (3:17), it is reported that the first man disobeyed his creator and the ground was cursed so that it brought forth only thorns and thistles. The passage sums up the feelings of most workers since the dawn of recorded time:

> Cursed is the ground for thy sake; in toil shalt thou eat of it all the days of thy life. . . . In the sweat of thy face shalt thou eat bread, till thou return to the ground.

The truth, I believe, is different. Research, experience, and common sense demonstrate that work itself motivates people and is a primary source of human dignity. Many workers have jobs they go to eagerly every day. They are the more fortunate ones. Their managers haven't removed all the motivating potential from the job itself. For them, staying away from the shop would be painful. All workers have days when they anticipate going to work with pleasure—often when they are completing a job that has challenged them, is important to the company, and promises them recognition for their efforts. Life has few higher prizes than this. A few workers have such interesting jobs that they prefer to be at the plant rather than at home.

It is not clear that managers have better jobs than workers. All work has the potential for satisfaction and achievement. What is clear is that managers spend more energy on enriching their jobs than on improving those in the shop. They have greater opportunities for removing the assumed stress and drudgery of work. It is characteristic of old-style companies that managers are protectionist rather than growth oriented. They have not gotten the message that work is the best source of self-stroking. When they do, they will restructure all work to maximize its motivational qualities. This is not to say there are not stupid, boring jobs. Such jobs should be automated as soon as possible. But even the worst jobs, if carefully structured, can be humanized.

WORK SATISFACTION

People want to work when work becomes a source of strokes. Work becomes a source of satisfaction when five things happen:

1. Workers have an opportunity to learn more, to stretch and grow. Monotony is painful. Accepting new challenges and facing new problems can be an invigorating experience for OK workers. There are few jobs that can't be improved by varying the nature of the task to provide continuous challenge and accomplishment. This is one of the benefits of pushing problems downward.

2. Responsibility flows from the freedom to make choices, plan, and organize. Contributing one's own ideas to the task by developing new tools, standards, and processes creates job ownership. To negate the worker's natural drive for responsibility and growth is to create repressed anger and frustration that will have baleful consequences on the job.

3. The motivational quality of achievement is contained in the apothegm "Nothing succeeds like success." Using one's skills to solve problems is a deep source of satisfaction. Accomplishment feeds a sense of vitality. It is no wonder new-style companies welcome employees' contributions to goal setting. In this they create the potential for achievement.

4. The natural consequence of success in an organization is receipt of recognition by the unit, its members, and its leaders. Most workers struggle in a stroke-starved economy. For them the rewards of achievement are highly valued. This explains the mysterious power of four inches of blue ribbon. Continuous reinforcing feedback is one of the distinguishing features of a new-style organization. Workers do not suffer from not knowing where they are in relation to the boss, other workers, and

the company's mission. Recognition is fundamental to this. There is great room for creative innovation in finding new ways to reward a job well done. I was pleased one afternoon to watch a manager in an insurance company make and distribute ice cream cones to the 100 or so denizens of his "papermill." He understood and benefited from his ability to give good strokes.

5. Integral to growth and recognition is the opportunity for advancement to higher challenges. Promotion is the ultimate reward for a job well done. It is the final demonstration of the company's commitment to its mission, its workers, and growth technology.

Work injustice is the consequence of workers' native Not OK feelings—their dimimished sense of self-worth, acceptance of pain related to work, drive for cooperation, and, finally, toleration of supervisory abuse. Abuse of workers by first-line managers is not uncommon in industry. The attempt of the Parent ego state to dominate others is ancient, and its consequences are almost always deleterious. Pointing it out brings a flood of rationalizations: "We've always done it that way." "You are too sensitive." "You do not understand our employees; they are used to it." "It's only shop talk." "The workers wouldn't know what to do if we were nice to them—they would suspect our motives." "They will think we've gone soft and take advantage of us." "We will lose control." "This isn't a church." "Nice guys finish last." The list goes on, ad nauseam. Abusive supervisors build distrust. It may be the single most debilitating thing for workers. Nobody benefits—not the company, the supervisor, or the worker.

Because workers will tolerate abuse, old-style managers feel confirmed in their cynicism, and craziness comes full circle. Everyone's negative expectations of everyone else are confirmed. The worst is not over. Unskilled managers may be encouraged to escalate their attacks. This increases worker resistance. As fight escalates, the classic symptoms of organizational malaise appear. Finally the police, prosecutor, or union organizers arrive. In the last case, as we have seen repeatedly, union leaders supplant plant managers as the people who really run things.

STRESS TECHNIQUES

Employee abuse is the behavioral part of work injustice. Old-style managers use stress techniques to control or defeat subordinates. Some leaders seek pain for others because of their own disturbed personalities. It's all part of their Not OK games with life. If their craziness is brought to their attention, they will compound it with inanity: "We've always done it this way."

What are some of the stress techniques old-style managers may from time to time employ? One common technique is diminishing others through shouting and cursing. This is particularly reprehensible when there is a vast power difference between the parties. Aggression against those over whom one has coercive power is unnecessary, rude, and inhuman. If the worker is likely to accept the abuse as true, it is more destructive. Who benefits by the corrosion of group trust and the destruction of workers?

Another common stress technique is withholding feedback from workers on the quality of their work, their position in the organization, and what direction the unit is moving. This can cause strong feelings of estrangement. If the organization does not accept responsibility for feelings of isolation, workers will form subgroups or countergroups for protection. It is a stimulating experience to work with employees who have high energy and a sense of mission because they know who and where they are and what the role of their unit is. Because they receive reinforcing feedback, they don't have to create anomalous groups to meet their emotional needs.

Part of the whole stress technique package is the willingness to tolerate hostile behavior as normal. When the gallows transaction receives social approval, the system withers. Attitudes of disdain, indifference, and hostility can easily become the norm. Then putdowns, games, dirty fighting, indifferent stares, obscene gestures, and hollow laughter are encouraged. When employees are trained in process management and are given the opportunity to create their own social environment, they will rid themselves of such behavior and substitute behavior that nourishes them and creates a sense of vitality.

Overloading willing individuals is another common stress technique. Old-style companies usually identify workers upon whom the entire operation seems to depend. These are the people who can be counted on in a crunch, and whose information is reliable; they are people who seem to value management's concerns. They are often conduits of information, counselors, and smoothers of troubled waters. In small companies this role is sometimes played by the president's secretary. Laying stress on willing soldiers is an easy thing to do. They become models for the wisdom "If you want a job done, ask a busy person." Sometimes this specialized responsibility devolves on the head of a key supervisor. Under ordinary conditions, the supervisor has a crucial linking position. The job is made doubly difficult when either or both parties are unskillful communicators or unrealistic in their demands.

The situation worsens when engineers set machine standards too tight, causing excessive worker fatigue and frustration. Industrial engineering is an excellent and often necessary management tool, useful in keeping costs down and productivity up. In the hands of callous or indifferent professionals, however, incentives can be used to abuse employees. Engineers concerned with work methods, material and equipment conditions, and operations seldom factor in social and spatial conditions. More and more we are discovering these have a profound influence on the business system. Time study experts have a rule of thumb for employee effort. They define it as "the amount of energy necessary to walk three miles per hour on straight and level ground without a load." Highly subjective in application, this rule allows great flexibility as to just what is a sound work standard. If unions become indifferent and engineers overzealous, standard setting can become a source of worker injustice.

Presumably easy to cure and yet a constant source of trouble is the refusal of first-line managers to listen to workers' complaints. If they heard them, doubtless they would correct them. Managers usually do what seems reasonable to correct worker complaints. Still there are exceptions. One shop I know of was organized because a faithful employee started having headaches when the late afternoon sun shone on the bright metal tools on his bench. Because of management's failure to listen and to provide a 75-cent shade, that company must now communicate to its employees through a third party. Such failure is the lifeblood of unionism. The message the employee gets from management is: "You are not important to us except as an appendage to a machine. We don't care whether or how you exist. Our contract with you is for your labor and if it pleases us we will pay you a fair wage." Employees who resist coercion and look for help are only showing their good sense.

Negative stereotyping—putting people down because of their membership in a class—is another stress technique. All workers have witnessed managers cursing or harassing subordinates because of their sex, race, religion, color, or some other condition they can do nothing about. Such abuse is rarely resisted. New-style management equips all workers to resist such behavior by creating norms that suppress it. Behavior is a function of the organization in which it occurs. If you change the culture of a company, you change member behavior. Only in the rarest instances will individual workers resist destructive behavior. Their need for membership is too strong and the bad feelings following separation are too painful.

Japanese corporations have demonstrated the high value of positive stereotyping. They create an upbeat management philosophy which they institutionalize in explicit ways. Arrogating "family" to the work organization and insisting that "all workers are brave and virtuous" is positive stereotyping. It benefits the workers and the company as a whole. Of course, if the message is phony, it won't work. The philosophy must be supported by a realistic salary and benefit program and by sound work rules and personnel policies.

Some companies accept hostile and attack behavior as the norm. When they tolerate behavior characteristic of the pre-scientific age, they handicap themselves in their ability to function in the new age. The substitution of fight for problem solving is an excess that an increasing number of companies indulge in.

The passion to win is useful only when it is put in the service of the Adult. Unfocused hostility corrodes group cohesion, disrupts communication, and confuses workers. Making members responsible for their jobs is the way to get through the thicket of rationalizations that protect old-style systems. Given the opportunity, employees will manage their own process in the direction of Nurturing Parent and Adult-based behavior. With top management support they will create a system of behavior that fits their work and social needs. Productivity and work integration will improve. Destructive behavior will die out and the work setting will become more rational and intuitive.

10

Performance Appraisal

Performance appraisal can have high motivational value. It offers an opportunity for both workers and supervisors to receive feedback, solve work problems, set new goals, and strengthen friendships. Admittedly these are difficult to achieve in an old-style Parent-Child context where management has not been trained in human behavior. Converting what is often a painful experience that both sides anticipate reluctantly into a high learning experience is one goal of a development program. The task is to turn a classic win-lose situation into a win-win learning opportunity. When performance appraisal is improved, wage and salary reviews become more realistic to employees.

THE VALUE OF APPRAISAL

There are four good reasons to continue the struggle to make performance appraisal work; all of them have the intention of developing people.

1. *Improving effectiveness.* Performance improvement is a major goal of appraisal. The appraiser seeks to assist the worker in fulfilling his or her desire for self-improvement and increased team productivity. If the worker still maintains an adversary position, this will have to be dealt with. Only when

workers trust the appraiser will there be space for them to accept responsibility for their own growth.

2. *Feedback on performance.* Not knowing where one stands in the eyes of superiors and peers can be a painful experience for a team member. Workers react to this no-communication situation either by adopting an "I don't need anybody" attitude or by screwing up. Since stroke deprivation is painful, in the absence of positive strokes workers will seek negative ones. As a minimum, the appraisal process ensures that no one goes too long without careful and consistent feedback. Each worker receives a careful assessment of his or her contribution to the total effort.

3. *Identifying development potential.* The appraisal process helps workers identify their potential for growth, their immediate goals, the ultimate level of work they desire, and the intermediate activities that prepare them for advancement. With this data, the appraiser can make human resources decisions about promotion, replacement, depth of management, and the like.

4. *Compensation.* Money is a motivator only when it is related to performance. The relationship between performance and compensation is often not clear in the worker's or manager's mind. Supervisors tend to distribute increases uniformly, with commendable desire not to hurt anyone. In failing to recognize or reward superior performance, however, supervisors foster mediocrity. Under an old-style system this makes some sense. But if you want to create a take-charge organization where workers play the game 100 percent, it is counterproductive. Money, as a motivator, has the quality of always going back to zero. Whether you're a mail clerk or a president, soon after your new raise you're likely to feel underpaid.

Relating compensation to appraisal makes the process more realistic to employees, stimulates learning, and, most importantly, rewards the stellar employee. This is consonant with the team-building process. It does not seek a little more friendliness, cooperation, and mannerliness. Assuming human elegance, it challenges performance of such a magnitude that it transforms both the organization and the worker. When this happens everyone will understand and value community. When workers play the game 100 percent, joy is restored to work.

BEHAVIOR TRAINING

Because appraisal is stressful for both parties, it is a great opportunity for game playing. In its simplest terms, a game involves two people denying with their behavior what they affirm verbally. Games are destructive and the antithesis of candor. All people have their favorite games, which they play when a suitable partner appears. Games can be ranked by the intensity of the players. First-degree games are common, accepted social rituals. They are the price of admission to the group. Second-degree games are more subtle. The players would prefer to keep a second-degree game hidden from view. If exposed, the game may result in embarrassment. Third-degree games are played for keeps and usually involve bodily harm.

A game starts when one player says one thing (a gambit) while meaning another. The respondent (mark) does not see the game and agrees with the con. Soon two people become involved in dirty fighting. At some point the con (oppressor) pulls a switch or cross-up and puts down the mark (oppressee). After the hoax is exposed, both players, if it is a first-degree game, shrug off the consequences with a variation of "Well, what did you expect? We are not running a party here." Once more the human enterprise is weakened and trust is annulled.

Hiring sometimes presents an opportunity for game playing. Below is an example, beginning with the prehire interview.

> BOSS: *(grimly)* We are all competitors here. Just
> work hard and keep your nose to the

grindstone, and you'll get along. We pay off
on results. If you're a good producer, you'll
get ahead. If you can't stand the heat,
well . . . .

NEW EMPLOYEE: (*determinedly*) You'll find I can take it and
give it out.

Almost one year later.

BOSS: (*bewildered*) I'm sorry but I'm going to have
to let you go. You just don't fit in. You've
upset almost everybody. Work isn't everything. You've got to have friends too.

The new employee was set up by the boss, who didn't tell him
the truth. He probably didn't know what it was. The employee
was mobilized to fight in a situation that didn't call for it. This
is a trapping game, because when the boss switched signals, he
not only was able to punish the new employee by firing him,
but could feel justified in doing so. Doubtless, that night the
boss went home and lamented to his wife about what a poor
crop of employees he'd been getting. If you'd watched the game,
you would have had no trouble separating the real from the
unreal. The payoff for the mark, by the way, is confirmation
that this is a dog-eat-dog world. Both boss and employee arose
the next morning to see if there weren't others to play their
game. And so it goes.

A first-degree game and its consequences are accepted by
everyone as normal for the situation. However, if a first-degree
game is played intensely, it may lead to a second- or even
third-degree consequence. After all, a game is really dirty
fighting.

The way to stop games is to tell the truth. The way to tell the
truth is to report where you are, what's so for you. This is not
hard. Heavy game players who have run their acts for a long
time may have trouble getting off them. They may have lost
touch or feel cynical about the possibility of support from any-

one else. The Adult is always there waiting to be turned on and has the potential to work perfectly. A valuable lesson of a development program is that telling the truth is liberating. When you report your feelings, ideas, and opinions as yours, you will interrupt games about you.

One more time: Games are dirty fighting. You can stop them by reporting what comes up for you. Game-free relations are transforming. Below are some classic performance appraisal games. The solid lines show the overt communication (con). The interrupted lines are the covert (real) message.

Gotcha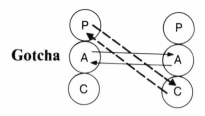

Surface Level

APPRAISER: (*with false warmth*) Well, George, it's that time of year again. You know I wouldn't bother with this sort of thing, but it is company policy.

APPRAISEE: Sure, I know they're always doing it to us.

APPRAISER: Now there are some things you can really improve on.

Hidden Level

Boss is about to punish. He feels free to do so because the company wants it. He is not accepting responsibility for his own behavior. The employee has been here before. He can expect no help from this appraiser. It is just part of the work game—another hurdle to go over, another putdown to be borne. The appraiser doesn't understand that reality is everyone's best friend. False friendliness is a lie: "I'm doing this for your own good." Or "If I don't punish you, soon everybody would be doing it." The Gotcha appraisal confirms people's cynicism and Not OK feelings.

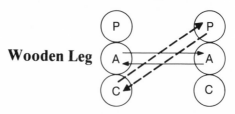

Wooden Leg

Surface Level

APPRAISEE: (*wheedling*) Why are you supervisors always on me? I certainly work as hard as the next guy. Why don't I get a break from you people? You expect everybody to be as interested in work as you are.

APPRAISER: I'm not always on you. But we have to make fewer mistakes in this department. And you make as many as anybody. Your attitude is not helpful.

APPRAISEE: Pick, pick, pick.

Hidden Level

Wooden Leg players view themselves as victims. Almost everyone around is dedicated to frustrating them. They plead special consideration, hoping to hook the careless into responding with sympathy or encouragement. "After all," they whine, "what do you expect from someone with a _____ (wooden leg)?" They don't see their own responsibility for the negative strokes they receive. The benefits of losing are enough for them to survive on. They have a sense of "Poor me, how the righteous suffer in the world." They can keep the we-they (labor-management) scam going. And usually they are able to distract others from the real task of work.

The way to interrupt the loser's game is to tell the truth. Talk directly to his Adult. Do not accept his self-derogation.

Point to his competence and intelligence. Recall his some-time higher self-expectations. Reality, not nurturance, is what the Wooden Leg player needs.

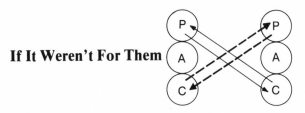

If It Weren't For Them

Surface Level

APPRAISEE: (*judgmentally*) How can I do my work when no-body else cooperates? Management won't give me proper tools, supervision sits on its hands, and others watch the clock all day.

APPRAISER: Sometimes it seems nobody gives a damn any-more.

APPRAISEE: I'm surprised this place runs at all.

Hidden Level

What do you do if you're stroke-starved and unable to take responsibility for what's going down? Blame others. All be-havior is reasonable and makes sense. No behavior means nothing. It is not always easy to see what's behind it. Depen-dency was a major consequence of old-style "putdown" man-agement. Workers were unconscious. They surrendered their sense of elegance and self to others' putdowns. Powered by Not OK, they waited for others to tell them what to do. They believed someone, somewhere, understood and controlled this mess.

"If It Weren't for Them" may be the hardest game to turn around. Workers know they're powerless. After that, blaming others makes sense. Restoring the concepts of individual participation, worker growth, and individual responsibility is what familial management is all about.

When employees can distinguish work-related behavior from other kinds of behavior, the horsepower of decision making will be increased. Workers' resistance will be reduced as they come to share ownership of organizational goals. When workers start succeeding, they won't even realize that they are no longer looking for a savior.

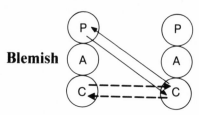

Blemish

Surface Level

APPRAISER: *(irately)* You have been trouble all year. If it's not one thing, it is another. It's people like you who give this place a bad name and encourage younger workers in poor habits. You're late too often . . .

APPRAISEE: *(sullenly)* I'm no worse than anybody else.

Hidden Level

The Blemish player has no trouble putting others in the wrong. Coming from his own Not OK position, he finds faults everywhere. He maintains his sense of being up by continually putting others down. He takes miserable pleasure in prying and snooping. He always talks down to people and never talks about the problem. He hopes his lack of knowledge and unwillingness to learn escape detection. Leadership for him is maintaining control by diminishing others. The likelihood of this succeeding in the new age is almost nil.

Blemish players see only what's inside themselves. There is

little or no correspondence between what they say and what is so. They are barely in touch with reality. They objectify their own attitudes. This very common mechanism, called projection, must be understood by those who attempt to appraise others. Knowing when people are talking about themselves and when they are talking about others is very important. Liberating the Adult, practicing "split attention," and owning their own feelings is the way Blemish players stop pushing responsibility on others. When this is done, they can begin to take effective control of their life and their work.

Ain't It Awful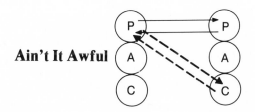

Surface Level

APPRAISER: (*disgustedly*) Things never let up around here. Doesn't it seem to you that people are different today? Nobody wants to work anymore. We're always fighting fires.

APPRAISEE: (*agreeably*) It's impossible to get work done because of the sea of paperwork. It takes me all morning to open my mail because the phone won't stop ringing. Then there are all those meetings. It's a wonder we get anything done around here.

Hidden Level

"Look what they're doing to us now." These two could go on indefinitely with their complaints. They derive miserable satisfaction from having so many misfortunes. "Nobody knows the trouble I've seen." Of course, by blaming others and lamenting their sad state they hope to be excused from not being on the problem. They hope to avoid the responsibility of thinking clearly and getting off their act. From someplace an Adult has to appear and call the game. "Let's get off it, guys, and get back to the problem at hand."

APPRAISAL RESULTS

Observation of the appraisal process and interviews with participants reveal that poor results are often the consequence of several factors:

1. *Appraisal unrelated to company's philosophy of management.* If each appraiser follows his or her private agenda, the program will have little meaning. If the process is not standardized across the company, it is not possible to make valid comparisons. Workers will attribute their results to the bad humor of their supervisors. To obviate this problem, management should train all those involved in both new-style values and basic ego state concepts. Standardization also makes the appraisal process a learning experience for both parties. Human potential is unlimited. The key to unlocking growth lies inside the worker. When workers discover mutuality and interdependence, the door will be open to learning.

2. *Poor communication skills.* An appraiser, precisely because he is in a power position, will have to be wary not to hook the appraisee's Not OK feelings of powerlessness. Prerequisite to good communication are mutual respect and caring. Both are dependent on the appraiser's ability to make authentic contact by giving strokes that the appraisee perceives as genuine. When both parties communicate—really share themselves—both will learn, stretch, and grow.

3. *Appraisal unfocused.* The appraiser must make adequate preparation. He needs to decide what he wants to discuss and

what changes might be made. Generalizations and opinions are not helpful. All discussions must be tied to concrete behavior. The process will be weakened if too many objectives are covered at one time. Suggestions for change should be limited to those the worker is able and ready to deal with.

4. *Lack of coaching and follow-up.* An annual or semiannual appraisal process must be supported daily with openness and concern. When a development contract has been made between appraiser and appraisee, it will be most effective if regular coaching takes place. The rule of recognition applies here: "Reward desirable behavior consistently and as soon as possible after it occurs. Overlook undesirable behavior as much as possible." The conclusion is inescapable that criticism has a negative effect on the achievement of goals. Rationally directed, long-lasting improvement proceeds by positive stroking. Coaching is a day-to-day activity.

PERFORMANCE APPRAISAL—TA INVENTORY

On the next few pages is a TA inventory of an employee's ego state availability compared with 18 standard business-related activities. Under each item in section A, the first answer reflects Parent scripting, the second an Adult here-and-now attitude, and the third a typical Adaptive Child response. Section B is an assessment of stroking skills, and section C is an inventory of the most common games played in business. This form can be used in conjunction with standard work-planning forms. The appraiser fills out the form and gives it to the employee a few days before the appraisal meeting. At the meeting the form is used as a basis for discussion. The appraiser need mark only those items he or she wishes to discuss. In every case the appraiser's position must be supported with reports of behavior the employee and others have seen. This is a measure of behavior or performance. Everyone can see behavior. It is now a subjective measure. The rules of effective feedback are as follows:

1. Describe the behavior fully and accurately.
2. Report the consequences to you in terms of your feelings. These effects can be tested with others.
3. Withhold conclusions, explanations, and judgments.
4. Give feedback as close to the event as possible.
5. Use feedback for learning, not for making others wrong.

PERFORMANCE APPRAISAL—TA INVENTORY

Name _____   Appraisal Period _____

Position _____   Department _____

A. For each item check the person's most characteristic behavior.

1. Goal setting
   ____Goals are set low to avoid resistance.
   ____Goals are set by consensus among those related to the problem. Past and future are considered.
   ____Little thought is given to goals.

2. Acceptance of orders
   ____Overtly accepted but covertly resisted.
   ____Accepted interdependence; disagreements openly discussed.
   ____"Anything you say boss" attitude.

3. Decision-making style
   ____Unilateral behavior because "I know best."
   ____All who can contribute to solution are given access to problem.
   ____Avoidance: "There's no problem so big I can't overlook it."

4. How time is spent on problems
   ____Shouts, threats, games, and politics substitute for problem solving.
   ____Thinking and problem-solving transactions are carried out between individuals and groups.
   ____Hard thinking is avoided through withdrawal, pastimes, rituals.

5. Discussion of individual behavior and group process
   ____Insists on status quo; tasks, not people, are important.
   ____Owns up to motivations; gives and receives helpful feedback.
   ____Is fearful and defensive; uses insights to trap others.

6. Willingness to share information with subordinates
   ____Manages by secrecy and threat.
   ____Shares freely; provides all information requested or explains refusal.
   ____Uses information for manipulative value.

7. Social distance between manager and subordinates
   ____Great distance; fears familiarity might reduce status and control.
   ____Little distance; group members are close and share many levels of their personality.
   ____Great distance; has Not OK feelings of helplessness.

PERFORMANCE APPRAISAL
(continued)

8. Use of control information
   ____Uses information largely to coerce, police, and punish.
   ____Uses information for self-control and for team guidance in problem solving.
   ____Ignores control information or uses it only to punish and "get even."

9. Expression of trust and confidence in subordinates
   ____Tends to see subordinates as incompetent and in need of direction.
   ____Is open and willing to take risks and share responsibility.
   ____Acts as if subordinates don't exist; expects them to be servile.

10. Expression of caring
    ____Is patronizing and ritualistic; puts people down.
    ____Is appropriately intimate in all situations; caring is legitimated.
    ____"Nobody cares about me, so why should I be concerned about others?"

11. Attitude toward conflict
    ____Conflict is seen as inevitable and agreement impossible; may even encourage conflict to look strong.
    ____Conflict is accepted, surfaced, identified, and resolved.
    ____Conflict is denied, repressed, and active beneath the surface.

12. Satisfaction derived from work
    ____Dissatisfaction arising from corrosive competition, destructive behavior, and stroke starvation.
    ____Satisfaction at all levels based on trust, participation, achievement, and recognition.
    ____Dissatisfaction and lack of a sense of achievement and recognition related to work.

13. Commitment to own professional growth
    ____Acculturated to organization.
    ____Committed to professional and interpersonal skill development.
    ____Overwhelmed by a sense of defeat and hopelessness.

14. Encouragement of professional training
    ____Uses training as a bonus for outstanding achievers; may see it as a potential threat.
    ____Assumes the organization can't grow if people don't grow.
    ____Sees training as a waste of time and money; uses it only to further narrowest company goals.

PERFORMANCE APPRAISAL
(continued)

15. Immediacy of feedback on performance
    ____Erratic, negating, and blaming.
    ____Immediate, direct, and consistent.
    ____Inconsistent, irregular, and threatening.

16. Performance appraisal as a learning experience
    ____Employee feels defensive, embarrassed, and "on the carpet."
    ____Engages in timely and mutual discussion of work issues and problems.
    ____Employee feels powerless and abused.

17. Characteristic transactions
    ____Punishing Parent to Child.
    ____Adult to Adult.
    ____Adaptive or Rebellious Child to Parent.

18. Nature of predominant transactions
    ____Judgmental, loud, and critical.
    ____Direct and friendly, fostering openness, trust, and confidence.
    ____Defensive with whining or blaming.

Score: Parent _____ Adult _____ Child _____

B. List examples of specific behavior under each heading.

1. Helpful/supportive behavior to self and others:

    _____
    _____
    _____
    _____
    _____
    _____

2. Hindering/discounting behavior to self and others:

    _____
    _____
    _____
    _____
    _____
    _____

PERFORMANCE APPRAISAL
(continued)

C. Check the games used by the employee. (Games are defined and diagramed in *TA and the Manager.*)

       _____Ain't It Awful
       _____Blemish
       _____Gotcha
       _____If It Weren't for Them
       _____I'm Only Trying To Help You
       _____Kick Me
       _____See What You Made Me Do
       _____Uproar
       _____Why Don't You . . . Yes, But
       _____Gee, You're Wonderful, Professor

D. Remarks:

Employee Signature   Date

Immediate Supervisor Signature   Date

WORK PLANNING

Although behavior training is necessary for individual development and team building, work planning is the heart of performance appraisal. Work planning means mutual goal setting. It affects the bottom line. Formal work planning may involve the entire organization, starting with the top and cascading down all levels. Beginning with a statement of purpose, major objectives are formulated and lesser, short-term goals are set for all segments of the company. The performance appraisal and midcourse correction points are established. The process is called management by objectives. For our purpose here, we shall discuss the single worker appraisal.

The objective of the entire process—training, completing appraisal forms, and scheduling—is to enable appraiser and employee to sit down and openly discuss the work they are jointly responsible for. When the discussion covers work issues that lead to new initiatives and is characterized by openness and trust, it is successful. The meeting should cover three areas: (1) report on past performance, (2) discussion of new ideas and initiatives, and (3) contracting.

The first part deals with output. How much productive work was actually turned out? What was the quality of the work? What was done to eliminate errors and reduce wasted resources? This phase includes the employee's response to supervision and ability to meet goals without direct supervision. Work safety performance, orderliness, and maintenance of equipment are also considered. Cooperation, support of others, and role on the team should be reported.

New ideas and methods are vital to the company's efforts to reduce costs. The second phase of the meeting deals with initiatives from the worker or supervisor to increase output, improve quality, redesign tools for products, and improve customer or government relations. The worker's ideas and initiatives should be dealt with seriously. Some can be implemented immediately on a trial basis. Others will need technical support that can readily be obtained. Still others will need serious consideration by higher authority. Casual or poorly thought-out ideas can be readily dismissed.

Contracting is the third phase of the appraisal meeting. Here measurable objectives are set and written down (see the Performance Planning Sheet). Action steps are listed along with the people responsible for them. These steps may include purchasing parts, attending a training course, defining new work methods, and securing technical help. Methods of measuring change are listed along with the time parameters.

To be effective, a contract must be agreed to by the worker's Natural Child. If the Adaptive Child is present, there will likely be resistance, reservations, quibble, and cavil. When transactions are Adult-monitored, easy, and agreeable, you can count on workers doing their best to keep their agreements.

For the supervisor, the contract becomes a task of monitoring and coaching. This can be done informally on a quarterly basis (see the Performance Appraisal Sheet). The process involves annually evaluating goals, rating overall performance, and making training and development recommendations.

Appraisals are often given on the worker's employment anniversary or are scheduled on one date for all members of the department. They are usually held once or twice a year but may occur more frequently if the situation demands it. After completing the form, the supervisor gives a copy to the employee at least three and not more than five days before the interview. This allows sufficient time for reflection but not enough to create stress.

The interview usually lasts an hour and is best held in a quiet, private place. Some shops have to make special effort to create a comfortable and quiet place. When both parties bring their Adult and OK Child to the meeting, it is pleasant and productive. When agreement is reached, it is recorded on the

Performance Appraisal Sheet and signed by both parties. There is space on the form for the worker to attach comments, agreements, and disagreements. The worker may also attach a letter to the form if he or she deems it desirable.

When disputes arise, third-party assistance can prove helpful. One large consumer products corporation has used outside assistance successfully for ten years. If workers feel they will not be treated fairly, they can ask for a third party to sit in. The third party's task is to maintain open communications by observing and commenting on process and behavior. The observer refrains from discussing substantative matters. The procedure helps to assure workers that their position is being heard and that they will receive fair treatment.

The Performance Planning Sheet and the Performance Appraisal Sheet appear on the following pages.

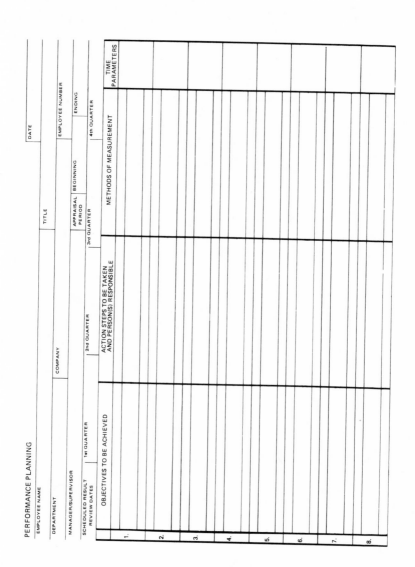

PROJECTED GROWTH

☐ INDIVIDUAL IS PROPERLY PLACED FOR THE FORESEEABLE FUTURE

☐ REASSIGNMENT SHOULD BE CONSIDERED FOR THE FOLLOWING REASONS

	TITLE	JOB CODE	DEPARTMENT
☐ EMPLOYEE WOULD LIKE TO BE CONSIDERED FOR			
	TITLE	JOB CODE	DEPARTMENT

☐ PROJECTED LOSS (DUE TO RETIREMENT, TRANSFER, RESIGNATION, OR DISMISSAL)

☐ INDIVIDUAL HAS POTENTIAL FOR ADVANCEMENT (IF CHECKED, FILL OUT EVALUATION OF POTENTIAL)

STEPS THAT HAVE BEEN TAKEN SINCE THE LAST PERFORMANCE APPRAISAL TO DEVELOP THIS INDIVIDUAL	STEPS THAT WILL BE TAKEN BEFORE THE NEXT PERFORMANCE APPRAISAL TO HELP DEVELOP THE INDIVIDUAL
1. ACTION TO BE TAKEN BY THE INDIVIDUAL	1. ACTION TO BE TAKEN BY THE INDIVIDUAL
2. ACTION TO BE TAKEN BY THE SUPERVISOR	2. ACTION TO BE TAKEN BY THE SUPERVISOR
3. WERE EXPECTED RESULTS ACHIEVED	3. RESULTS EXPECTED

CURRENT JOB — TRAINING AND DEVELOPMENT RECOMMENDATIONS

FORMAL OR CROSS TRAINING RECOMMENDED TO IMPROVE ON-THE-JOB PROFICIENCY	TRAINING COURSE CODE

GENERAL COMMENTS

INCLUDE STATEMENTS HERE FOR CLARIFICATION OF ANY SECTION WHERE FURTHER INFORMATION WOULD BE DESIRABLE. IN ADDITION INCLUDE MAJOR OR UNUSUAL ACCOMPLISHMENTS SINCE THE LAST APPRAISAL AND LIST NEW OBJECTIVES TO BE ACCOMPLISHED IN THE NEXT YEAR. USE ADDITIONAL SHEETS IF NECESSARY.

PREPARED BY	TITLE	DATE	EMPLOYEE'S SIGNATURE (DENOTES UNDERSTANDING NOT NECESSARILY AGREEMENT)	DATE	RECOMMENDED NEXT REVIEW
APPROVED	TITLE	DATE	REVIEWED BY	TITLE	DATE

EMPLOYEE'S COMMENTS

PERFORMANCE APPRAISAL

NON-EXEMPT	EXEMPT	DEPARTMENT		APPRAISAL DATE
EMPLOYEE'S NAME	EMPLOYEE NO.	TITLE	COMPANY	
COST CENTER	HIRE DATE	DATE OF LAST INCREASE	AMOUNT OF INCREASE	SCHEDULED DATE OF	JOB CODE	SALARY GRADE

In the first column list the major objectives which were established in the Performance Planning Session and subsequent Progress Reviews. Utilizing this information and Fourth Quarter Accomplishment Report, list the results achieved. Use additional sheets if necessary.

THE PERFORMANCE PLAN WAS REVIEWED AND UPDATED ON (DATES)	1st QUARTER	2nd QUARTER	3rd QUARTER	4th QUARTER/ACCOMPLISHMENT REVIEW
OBJECTIVES ESTABLISHED			RESULTS ACHIEVED	

EVALUATION OF CURRENT PERFORMANCE

OVERALL PERFORMANCE RATING

POOR	FAIR	COMPETENT	EXCELLENT	SUPERIOR

BENEFITS (value to organization tangible & intangible)

ALTERNATIVES AND THEIR CONSEQUENCES (other means of accomplishing goals and effects of not achieving)

RESOURCES REQUIRED (capital and expense dollars, man-hours/days/assistance needed, space, and equipment)

EMPLOYEE SIGNATURE   DATE

SUPERVISOR SIGNATURE   DATE

Index